10 1/16"

New Southern Classicism

The Residential Architecture of Barry Fox

New Southern Classicism

The Residential Architecture of Barry Fox

Philip Kopper

Martin & St. Martin
Publishing Company

New Orleans ♦ Savannah
A GOLDEN COAST BOOK

For additional information contact
Barry Fox Associates, Architects, Ltd.
1519 Washington Avenue, New Orleans, LA 70130
504/897-6989

Designed, produced, and distributed by Golden Coast Publishing Company, Savannah, Georgia.
www.goldencoastbooks.com.

PHOTOGRAPHY
© Robert S. Brantley: 12, 17/bottom, 18/all, 19/center and bottom, 28, 30–33, 34/top, 35–37, 38/top, 39, 40–43, 46–47, 50,
51/left, 56–61, 70–75, 76–81, 84–87, 107/top, 124–26, 128–31, 133–37, 139–41, 144/bottom, 144/right, 176, 178, 182–83,
185, 187–91, 192–95, 196–97, 198/top, 199–201, 211, 212/bottom left and right, 218–19, 221–25, 238–41, 243–47, 248, 250;
© Jan White Brantley: 17/center, 20/top
© Hickey-Robertson: 34/bottom, 38/bottom left and right;
© Koch and Wilson, Architects: 17/top;
© James R. Lockhart: 2 (title page), 44, 48–49, 51/right, 52–55, 62–69, 138, 142–43, 144/top, 146,
148–53, 210, 213–17, 226–35;
© Van Jones Martin: 6 (contents), 23, 26–27, 88–91, 94–103, 112, 114–16, 118–23,
154–63, 166–75, 202–08;
© David Spielman: ix;
© Dominique Vorillon: 104/bottom, 105-06, 108-11;
Private Collection: 14/top and bottom, 15/top and center, 16/all, 132;
Library of Congress, Historic American Buildings Survey: 15/bottom.

Drawing on page 19 © George Schmidt.
Color renderings on pages 29, 82, 104, 184, 212, 236-37 © Edgar Smith.

Edited by Jane Powers Weldon and Douglas Lewis.
Design assistance by Jo Morrell.
Color separations by Savannah Color Separations, Inc., Savannah, Georgia.
Printed in China by Bookbuilders through Asia Pacific Offset, Inc.

Endsheet illustration: Full-scale column detail.
Title page photograph: Nelson portico, New Orleans.
Contents page photograph: Anderson entrance/stair hall, Jacksonville, Florida.

ISBN 0-932958-26-5
Library of Congress Control Number: 2006927497

The publishers dedicate this book to
the gracious owners of the homes featured within these pages.
Without their hospitality this project would not have been possible.

Contents

Preface

PAUL ST. MARTIN is the catalyst that allowed this book to be published. Having a keen appreciation for classical architecture, and in particular the work of Andrea Palladio, Paul has made it his mission to bring public awareness to the wealth of twentieth-century classical architecture to be found in the Deep South. This body of architectural richness springs from the drawing boards of architects specializing in classical design practicing from the early 1920s into the present. Paul deserves my depth of gratitude for including the work of our firm in this distinguished group.

Van Jones Martin of Savannah provided the technical expertise in putting this book together. His varied talents, architectural photography, editing, and layout make for a perfect fit with Paul's vision.

Author Philip Kopper provided an enlightening perspective into the delicate relationships that architects encounter in what invariably becomes a close partnership between client and designer.

I am grateful for the creativity of three very distinguished architectural photographers, Van Jones Martin, Jim Lockhart, and Robert Brantley, working in what is slowly becoming the lost art of large format color photography. David Kaminsky deserves credit for his technical work in translating the various media of the photographs, drawings, renderings, and plans into the striking images on these pages. I would also thank David Spielman for additional photographic assistance.

My very special thanks go to Frank W. Masson, AIA, who for years has been by my side in assisting on these residences. He has provided invaluable design support, and I marvel at his enduring love of the precise architectural detail. I am proud that the publishers have included as part of this book a sample of three incredible residences for which he was the architect.

The residences that the publishers selected for this book would not have been possible without the able assistance of my staff, associates Glenn Carriere, Van Jenkins, Dale Burke, and Amanda Shepherd. To my assistant Holly LaBarre, I owe a deep appreciation for her administration of our office and for her enduring loyalty.

Other former associates that I feel deserve special recognition are Lewis Robinson, James Cripps, Adrian Callais, Jesse Daniels, Rob Segura, Rob Smith, and Ames Yates.

New Orleans has been blessed for generations with a plethora of quality artisans and craftsmen, a tradition that has often been handed down from father to son and then to grandson.

In the woodworking trade, the Hartdegen brothers, Jason and Clayton, have followed their father, Gus, in crafting from our full-size drawings magnificent wood doors, windows, frames, casings, cornices, pediments, balustrades, cabinetry, paneled rooms, and fine custom staircases. Others with whom our firm has collaborated over the years have been Alex Kondroik, Scanlon-Taylor, Bill Rainey, and Mike Ellis.

The Tevis Vandergriffs, father and son, continue the almost lost trade of creating exquisite hand-fashioned moldings and cornices on site in wet plaster or stucco. Tommy Lachin and his dad, Albert, and grandfather Victor have taken their Italian heritage in stonecutting, cast stone, and cast plaster to a high level of perfection. Others practicing in cast plaster and composite ornament of decorative designs that are unique to New Orleans are Janusz Urbanski and Beth Delbert. Lionel and Lonnie Smith, father and son, work in sheet metal and slate, tile, and most any eighteenth- or nineteenth-century roof material. In Baton Rouge, Walter Smiley, and in Lakeland, Florida, Barry Huber are special roofing and slaters who deserve recognition. Richard Wood has been a source for decades for fine recycled old heart pine, oak, and exotic species of flooring and paneling.

Stonemasons who have contributed to the quality of our residences are Teddy Pierre Jr. and Sr., Pete Tucker, John Carr, and Mario Lovisa.

Among the many competent iron fabricators with whom we have had the privilege to work are Vic Eumont, Sid Lou, and Don and Alan Tudury.

Several ornament painters with whom I am proud to have been associated are the John Geisers (father and son), Keith Guy, Chris Landers, Darren Brunet, and Taylor Livingston.

A special thanks goes to the New York designer Sam Blount for his remarkable interiors and to local designers Gerrie Bremermann, Sue Menge, and the late Lucille Andrus.

Finally I want to give my thanks to my children Barry Jr. and Elizabeth and especially to my wife, Maxine, for their constant encouragement and support in my architectural career.

Barry Fox

Foreword

THERE IS A SERIES OF FASCINATING PARALLELS between the works (as celebrated in this book) by Barry Fox of New Orleans (1938–) and those by the greatest architect of the affluent Edwardians, Sir Edwin Lutyens of England (1869–1944). Lutyens was a genius of assimilation, and his greatest gift was to assemble evocative references to earlier styles, in picturesque ensembles of great natural charm—incorporating interiors of brilliantly modern efficiency but also of luxuriously detailed comfort. To Americans his best-known work may well be his extraordinarily splendid residence for the British embassy in Washington, at the highest point of the Massachusetts Avenue axis adjoining the vice-president's house at Observatory Circle. In the form of a vast country house set in a large, verdant park, that fabulous creation presents a breathtaking silhouette of astonishing variety, whose wing connections and terminal pavilions, with courtyards, drives, and gatehouses, all build with unusual confidence and mastery toward a triumphantly festive central block, making the ensemble's complex exploration a continuous delight. Lutyens got his start in 1896 with Munstead Wood House in Surrey, an eclectic masterpiece somewhat in the Norman farmhouse or Queen Anne Revival styles of the great eclectic architect of the preceding generation, Norman Shaw; he went on to design the imperial-revival British School at Rome and most famously the viceroy's house at New Delhi in India, an enormous enterprise that occupied him

Barry Fox at home in New Orleans.

throughout the second and third decades of the twentieth century.

Barry Fox is noted only once in the text of this book as explicitly acknowledging an influence from Lutyens, in his inspiration for an Anglophilic sort of Norman farmhouse of his own, the rambling, essentially one-story, and picturesquely composed Svendson House (1998) in Baton Rouge; but almost every page of this beautiful book suggests further connections. Lutyens contributed to a famous book of 1925 by Nathaniel Lloyd, *The History of English Brickwork*; Barry Fox has been so attentive to the importance of that medium as to have bricks handmade especially for his buildings (as for example in the lustrous Flemish-bond walls of his Doby House of 1993 in Madison County, Mississippi, which startlingly recreates the style of Wilton House at Richmond or the George Wythe House at Williamsburg). There are Fox designs of such varied silhouette and planimetric grandeur as to recall Lutyens specifically, such as his own version of an enormous Colonial Revival country house for the Edward Dobbs family in Atlanta (1994); but more centrally it is the sheer delight in the entire previous history of grand domestic architecture that most tellingly connects these two eclectic masters. For Fox, of course, that history is now a century longer than it was for Lutyens; and, crucially, it also has the advantage of including as well the personal works by that previous kindred spirit, as a constant inspiration to stretch the confines of the domestic envelope.

And stretch them Fox certainly does. There are indeed a few predictably deft small designs for restricted sites or programs in the two dozen commissions by Barry Fox that are showcased in this book (whose twenty-seven projects include twenty-four by Fox and three—among them some of the finest small-scale work, in the French Quarter or the Faubourg Marigny—by his brilliant associate Frank Masson); but mostly these are large-scale country or suburban houses for comfortably well-off patrons of the New South, about whom Philip Kopper writes so provocatively in this text. Fox's most favored configuration, a unilinear five-part plan with a tall central block flanked by the recessed "hyphens" of low wing passages, culminating in projecting terminal pavilions, is one whose Renaissance, late Baroque, and neoclassical ancestry deserves further elucidation. That classic five-part configuration (historically expressed almost identically on a land, approach, or street façade, as it was also similarly rendered on an opposite water, park, or garden façade) is often called Palladian; but Andrea

Palladio himself (Italian, 1508–80) is essentially innocent of its invention. The nearest approximations of that eventual northern European and American type to appear in the Renaissance oeuvre of that "most imitated architect in history" (as James Ackerman called him in 1967) are very differently scaled and proportioned: Palladio's Villa Barbaro at Maser (1554–58) or Villa Emo at Fanzolo (c. 1565–67), for example, have that basic outline, but their connecting wings are far longer than their central blocks are wide, and their terminal elements are merely modest-sized dovecotes, placed atop those long south-facing arcades. Palladio's Villa Pisani at Montagnana (1552–55), more interestingly, indeed has a tall, cubic, central block and was planned to have recessed hyphens, in the form of lower arches over a road and private drive, connecting to large end pavilions, intended for staff and service functions; but the latter four elements were never built. Thus it came about that on the basis of seventeenth-century prototypes (rather than sixteenth-century ones) for less sunny lands, by northern Baroque masters such as Inigo Jones, Sir Christopher Wren, and Sir John Vanbrugh, it fell to the English neo-Palladianists of the early eighteenth century, under the leadership of Richard, Earl of Burlington (1694–1753), to perfect the five-part country-house plan with short, enclosed hyphens and complex end pavilions. In the hands of the many associates and followers of that committed Palladian revivalist—especially Campbell, Flitcroft, Richardson, Paine, and eventually, above all, the brothers Adam—this classic configuration reached a truly heroic scale, as well as an almost neo-imperial complexity; but more modest five-part compositions were also exported to the American colonies and early republic through the publications of Lord Burlington's circle (most especially in the handbook of affordable plans by Robert Morris) and flourished along the whole length of the Atlantic seaboard. The type is most famously represented in America by the great James River compositions of Westover and Carter's Grove, attributed to Richard Tagliaferro, as colonial examples from the middle decades of the eighteenth century. Benjamin Henry Latrobe's Riverdale, of just after 1800 for the Calvert family in suburban Maryland, is a canonical neoclassical example; while Gore Place, of about the same date and probably by Charles Bulfinch, in the exurbs of Boston, is a shining specimen (with its oval rooms and interlocking floor levels) of more imaginative planning on the five-part theme, as it is exemplified in the highly original designs of Barry Fox.

The first consideration that one notices, in assessing the basic configurations of Fox's most elaborate county-house plans, is how frequently the central block is extruded out of its historical cubic shape, and how freely the flanking elements are conceived. Fox's central reception rooms are characteristically organized around a principle of vertical integration, or a radial axis, often culminating in a central octagon, rotunda, or belvedere-with-oculus. The interaction of that vertical organization (involving, on the façades, a variety of portico types and pyramidal roof treatments), with the linear, straight-line extension of the five-part plan, typically offers Fox a series of creative tensions that are frequently resolved (as at Gore Place two hundred years ago) by interleaved floor levels, rooms pulled out of conventional rectangles into centralized plans, and above all by a highly unpredictable—but enormously appealing—eccentricity in the massing, height, and articulation of the flanking blocks. In the case of the water façade of his Howe Residence of 1996 in coastal South Carolina, for instance, the octagonal corner pavilions attached to the extreme edges of the central block artfully recall one of the most revered prototypes of Tidewater architecture, the same curious corner pavilions at Mulberry Plantation, from the earliest years of the eighteenth century. As Philip Kopper has repeatedly observed in this text, it is exactly that confident and almost casual (but always carefully considered) reference to regional prototypes and historic precedents that gives Fox's work its impressive aura of authenticity.

Another element that commands both the intellectual respect of critics and also (more importantly) the logistical gratitude of patrons is Barry Fox's willingness to assimilate new architectural functions. The flanking masses of his five-part plans, especially—but also, just as frequently, the "classic" reception rooms at a house's core—are configured for uses as novel and divergent (from historical "norms") as exercise rooms, media rooms, mud rooms, wine rooms, computer offices (quite separate from offices for clients, or studies, or libraries, and in quite unpredictable—but compellingly functional—parts of the house), and many other twenty-first-century functions. That such activities can be woven seamlessly into a classically articulated whole (with elaborate crown cornices, as one bemused father-in-law observed, even in the kitchen) is a high tribute to Fox's creative imagination, but also to his overriding sense of decorum. That latter attribute establishes its own, internal cre-

ative tension, with his equally broad-minded admiration of ornament. Barry Fox's meticulous, accurate, and always historically appropriate ornamentation is one of the touchstones of his success; equally, it helps to define his place in the history of architecture. The arid monotonies of the self-impoverished International Style, in the "modernist" movement of the mid-twentieth century, inspired in reaction the sometimes whimsical excesses of Postmodern architecture, with its casually tongue-in-cheek references to older styles, overlaid (for the most part) on essentially the same stripped-style structures. Barry Fox's much sounder, more solidly based, and more admirable talent is to stretch the very skeletons of historical types into new celebrations of the complexity of contemporary life, and to unify those sometimes dissonant harmonies through a precision of ornamental enrichment—in order to achieve, as in the masterpieces of Lutyens, solutions whose balanced complexities can inspire a lifelong delight.

Who knows what the future still holds for Barry Fox Associates? Lutyens, after all, was called late in life to help design a whole new framework for the British Raj, and made it his masterpiece. Might it be too much to hope that our contemporary opportunity for a truly serious reconfiguration of New Orleans (as emerging in the aftermath of Hurricane Katrina, of late 2005) may possibly offer certain parallel potentialities to Barry Fox?

Douglas Lewis, Ph.D., F.A.A.R.
New Orleans, June 15, 2006

Introduction

Gulf view from widow's walk.

THE BOLD WHITE HOUSE towering over acres of storm wreckage, beach sand, and leafless live oaks rises three floors to its crown: the belvedere, a cupola surrounded by a wide widow's walk, which commands the noble view of the barrier islands and the Gulf of Mexico stretching to the horizon. One imagines an antebellum belle, with her parasol, pacing behind the balustrade sixty feet in the air, passing a whole sad day watching her cavalier's ship telescoping away, outward bound, hull-down, then out of sight; or during the War for Southern Independence a Confederate lookout at this lofty post signaling to a blockade runner still leagues offshore as it beats for safety within the Mississippi delta. *One imagines . . .* as if this height had been erected two centuries ago. But it wasn't.

Viewed from the ground, the belvedere, though big enough for a bridge party or billiards, looks as perfectly proportioned as the finial atop a Chippendale chest-on-chest would in the elegant parlor below, with its thirteen-foot ceilings and white walls awaiting Mr. Audubon's huge folio likenesses of our native birds. But when visitors climb the circular staircase—itself a work of art, with corkscrew mahogany banister and hand-sawn pine treads—they are reminded by the sight of a Jacuzzi and multiple telephone jacks in the upstairs study that this large dwelling was not here long ago. In fact its construction began in the twenty-first century. Yet once it is built and inhabited, and the contractors' and Katrina's debris trucked away, and new date palms planted, some passersby may take this house for an ancient landmark as readily as they take *Gone with the Wind* to be true history. "They sure knew how to build them in the old days," a sightseer might say, not knowing that this new house survived the terrible hurricane of 2005 thanks to some well-planned applications of modern construction that might wisely be replicated elsewhere. But more of that in my epilogue.

The house overlooking the coast road at Pass Christian, Mississippi, appears in some respects as actually antique as Tara must have been in Margaret Mitchell's mind. More to the point, it is an elegant dwelling conceived both to reflect a regional esthetic and to provide every modern amenity for a prosperous, three-generation family of New South gentry. You might say it was designed both to nurture selected old traditions and to accommodate a very *now* lifestyle—given that both the architect who conceived this place and the people who will dwell here all live and breathe today, early in the third millennium.

In some visual features the residence on the Gulf represents the finest of revived and recalled classical styles: Greek Revival first and foremost, while some motifs are pure Palladian, some Anglo-Caribbean, some Federal, and some features absolutely up-to-the-minute contemporary, such as the electric passenger elevator and remote-controlled garage doors enclosing space to park a half-dozen cars. In physical terms, the house blends modern and antique elements: the cutting-edge fire suppression system and the banister scarfed together by a master carpenter from three hundred blocks of mahogany, the traditional foot-and-a-half-deep crown moldings laid up in wet plaster in the time-proven manner by a team of master plasterers, and the plasma TV screen that nests out of sight beneath a marble slab when not showing Ole Miss games to the cheering clan. In sum, this residence is a glittering example of a new southern classic, an aggressive, pragmatic, hybrid architectural genre.

This eclectic mode, the stylistic specialty of the New Orleans architect Barry Fox, is neither Classical Revival nor *historical* (i.e., not any formal order that thrived in a specific period). Rather, Fox combines distinct elements that reflect distinct styles and tastes of different bygone eras. Like southern culture itself, which blends an alphabet of legacies from Acadia to Yazoo and Yoknapatawpha County, this architecture revels in its eclecticism: variously harmonious, contrapuntal, and dissonant. A Barry Fox residence—which may most resemble a Federal townhouse or Italianate villa, a Norman farmstead, Creole plantation, or Regency duplex—does not express an Old South vernacular redolent with the graces and paces of agrarian life when cotton was king. Rather, his traditional residences somehow reflect a brash modern Dixie, the twenty-first-century region that glories in the rough-and-tumble of high-tech engineering, space-age commerce, and venture capitalism that makes fortunes at the speed of light—a modern Dixie of active recreations and flamboyant amusements that also cherishes its romantic past.

In Fox's hands, a client's residence blends the gracious charms and classical proportions of older eras into new forms, some of them larger than their antecedents by an order of magnitude, perhaps to reflect today's heartier appetites for life and the resources that sustain them. Neither shy nor modest, this architecture proudly resonates aspects of a remembered or imagined Old Deep South as it celebrates the highly energized Grand New South through a new synthesis in the dialectic of design. This architecture may itself be read as an expression of its place and time.

Further, Barry Fox's contributions to this originally reminiscent style, and to modern residential building, represent an acme of that new synthesis, an apotheosis within the contemporary genre. As he borrows visual elements from the region's manifold past and combines them to augment each other, he melds them into near-orders of new building styles that all share a program (in the architectural sense of the term). A residence designed by Barry Fox's firm appears to have three principal traits: rarely understated, in overall appearance it evokes a traditional or period style; in both exterior form and countless interior vignettes, it displays an extraordinary attention to historically inspired detail; and in each building's program it comfortably provides all manner of modern amenities such as a home movie theater, exercise suite, and state-of-the-art appliances to accommodate a range of activities that suits the particular client family's manner of living.

As dominant themes and styles vary from house to house, there is even a degree of magical variation in a Fox design when, for instance, the front elevation of the new house at Pass Christian presents a Greek Revival façade to the passing stranger on the public road, while from the private acres in the rear it appears more English, almost purely Georgian, a tribute to the esthetic legacy of Hanoverian Britain. Similarly a rambling residence built for a Minnesota family on the banks of Florida's St. Johns River has the look of a Caribbean sugar plantation from the waterside and that of a great Tidewater manor from the landward approach; thus it seems a distinguished residence in the classic Georgian style that came from Britain and evolved in her southern American colonies into a style of grand building defined by five parts: the central mass flanked symmetrically on either side by a wing made of two sections. In both these instances, as in many others, the marriage of elements of distinct architectural styles appears a happy union, quite possibly because of a trait that satisfied clients invariably mention in passing: Barry Fox's innate sense of proportion. He gets the proportions *right*—in the shape of a room, the slope of a roof, and the height of a column beneath its pediment.

Farther down the St. Johns River stands a house that can be best described as "Jeffersonian" in its distinct atavism, its reverent echoes of Monticello. Fittingly, its rotunda features a pair of doors that open and close simultaneously, driven by unseen machinery based on a design by Thomas Jefferson himself. This room is illuminated by a new device equally deft in its high-tech contrivance: natural light shines down through a unique structure of laminated glass in the cupola overhead (of which more later).

One common denominator shared by all these houses is profuse elegance. Another is the beauty that arises from a remarkable coefficient of detail—an astonishing attention to individual elements, which combine in that previous asset, the obvious elegance, as amassed details add up to more than the sums of their parts. Virtually every Barry Fox house features such niceties as these: stone floors and parquet done in two contrasting woods; a ground floor plan driven by the residents' intention to entertain that lets parties flow outside from living room to garden and back again through French doors or triple-hung windows; wall panel cabinetry and joinery worthy of fine furniture; paneled walls and custom doors crafted in scarce and beautiful woods such as sinker cypress harvested from the bottoms of rivers and swamps and heart pine salvaged from eighteenth- and nineteenth-century industrial buildings; perfect marble pavers in a hallway (where they are seen up close) but exterior decorations (which are seen from farther away) of Indiana limestone or cast in plaster, fiberglass, and resin to simulate stone; here a Diocletian window, there a cornice of triglyphs, bucranes (ox skulls draped with garlands), and egg-and-dart designs borrowed from classical motifs; a kitchen equipped for professionals' use (whether the lady of the house cooks or depends on caterers); a potting shed for the gardener in the family; a carpentry shop for the hobbyist; a gym with sauna and shower hidden under a mansard roof; Ionic columns and Palladian windows perfectly modeled on antique originals; a wrought-iron fence and gate on its original granite base recycled from the earlier house on the site where the new house stands. The list of acquired elements goes on.

◆　◆　◆

As his southern classic architecture represents the region of its origins, the New South classicist himself proudly has southern roots. Barry Fox is the scion of a New Orleans family that prospered with the success of a grain export enterprise founded by his grandfather, Crichton Beresford Fox. Family lore traces its ancestry to John Beresford, the first Earl of Tyrone in Waterford, who was named King George III's commissioner of revenue in 1780 and who hired James Gandon to build the customs house in Dublin called Beresford House. Crichton's father, born in England, became a wine merchant and moved the family to Le Havre where Crichton grew up. After his father's death, Crichton left France about 1890, picking New Orleans as the place to seek his fortune because his fluency in French might be useful. Indeed the young immigrant married Bertha Pitot, whose first language was French, a granddaughter of New Orleans's first mayor, James Pitot. She always preferred the romance language to English, and perforce her household was bilingual, to her grandson's fascination. Barry remembers as a boy asking his grandmother after she returned from her weekly confession, "Do you sin in French too?"

Born in New Orleans in 1938, Barry spent his teenage years in Metairie, a select neighborhood established a generation earlier as the city's "first" upriver suburb just beyond the pales of central Orleans Parish. He went to Metairie Park Country Day School, a "progressive" private school that emphasized the arts, fostered creativity, and prided itself on culturally enriching curricula. Barry found pleasure and success in drawing, painting, sculpture, pottery, and such artistic subjects. When he was on the cusp of adolescence, his parents happened to

Above: Portrait of John Beresford (1738–1805), by Gilbert Stuart in 1790. Below: Foxhall, c. 1750, near Legan, County Longford, Ireland.

enable a priceless awakening by hiring the dean of the Tulane Architecture School, John Lawrence, to design a 1950s contemporary home for them. The evolving plans for the house captivated the boy; then the curious pictures called blueprints opened a new world for him when he watched them become manifest as walls and windows, floors and roof. When he worked one summer as a laborer on the site, he began to learn rough carpentry and the arts of actual building.

He found another source of fascination far from the new house that would be his home and the antique city that surrounded him from September to June. Going off for two summers with an outfit called the Prairie Trek Expedition, a peripatetic boys' camping program in the Southwest, he experienced an epiphany. The campers toured in pickup trucks around the Four Corners (where Colorado, Utah, Arizona, and New Mexico meet) with counselors who were experts, or grad students at least, in arcane fields. Here Barry became intrigued by the prehistoric cultures of the high desert, erstwhile territory of the vanished Anasazi and their successors, the living Hopi and Navajo whose woven baskets intrigued him. With their tutors/drivers/guides, the boys found unmarked sites of ancient settlements and did their own "archaeology"—digging, cataloging, and photographing their finds. Barry became especially interested in the ancients' spectacular (if sometimes tiny) cliff dwellings and the curious, round, ceremonial chambers that are now called kivas and are still very much in use. Returning home in the fall, he declared his ambition to become an archaeologist. His father, a practical businessman who regretted not having himself trained for one of the higher professions, said, "Who's going to be your patron?"

At Metairie Park Country Day, Barry remembers focusing on the visual and manual arts as well as math and science. In his senior year he was told he might follow his father to college at Princeton (as his brother would). Instead he happily chose Washington and Lee University, where he started to study engineering until he lost interest in the math and gained new interest in the fine arts thanks to an inspiring teacher. After two years in Lexington, Virginia, he transferred home to study in the architecture school at Tulane under the dean, the family friend and architect John Lawrence. It was tough, he recalls, with design labs every afternoon, but the first semester involved lots of drawing—everything from nudes to buildings and landscapes—as well as making models and design per se. Barry found himself thoroughly engaged.

Prairie Trek Expedition top and above: Young Barry Fox on horseback and Barry Fox's photograph of a Native American archaeological site, showing circular kivas. Below: The "Colonnade" at Washington and Lee was an inspiration for a career in architecture.

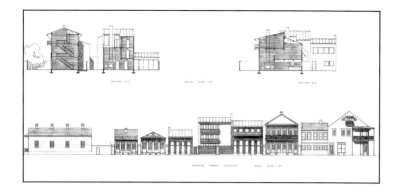

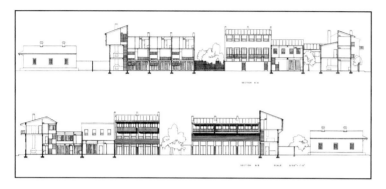

Barry Fox's final thesis for Tulane University School of Architecture portraying contemporary residential infill within the context of a historic block in the Vieux Carré. Elevations, sections, and detail drawings.

Offered the opportunity to be the first architecture student to participate in Tulane's foreign exchange program, he says he considered London's Architecture Association School and the New Bauhaus at Ulm in southern Germany, then chose Scotland for his fourth year. At the University of Edinburgh he studied with the dean of the School of Architecture, the distinguished Scottish architect Sir Robert Matthew, designer of London's Royal Opera House. His sojourn there offered another surprise opportunity: a tutorial with the internationally acclaimed American architect Louis Kahn, who came to Scotland to study castles and advance his "bi-nuclear" plan of designing buildings with multiple focal points. This exposure would have lasting effects in Barry's work, in such residences as the J. F. Bryan home in Jacksonville and the Foster Walker summer residence near Cashiers, North Carolina, where construction began in 2005.

Pedagogy in Edinburgh revolved around small classes of about a dozen students and lengthy discussions of diverse topics: history, art, the theory of architecture, and—given their locus—"historical contextualism" in a city whose New Town dated from the eighteenth century and Old Town from seven centuries earlier. In Sir Robert's view, urban buildings were vital parts of a living organism: when an old tooth was gone, the new tooth had to fit the space; when an old building was replaced, the new one had to look as if it belonged there. Discussion with tutors and fellow students went on endlessly, often after hours in the Abbotsford Pub, a hangout for architects, poets, and men of letters. There was not as much practical design work as Tulane offered; rather here was a team approach to diverse projects in one Scottish vernacular or another, whether antique restorations along historic Princes Street or new tracts of council houses at the city's expanding edges. And within all was the new pervasive spirit of Kahn's adventurous Modernism and inquisitive atavism as he studied older styles of architecture and adapted them into new syntheses.

Returning to New Orleans in the fall of 1962, Barry used his Scotland experiences to mold his senior thesis, a residential infill of modern architecture in the historic Vieux Carré, the French Quarter. Upon graduation Barry began his career in the firm of Koch and Wilson, architects to the carriage trade. Samuel Wilson, Jr., the more academic partner and teacher of a popular course in the history of Louisiana architecture at Tulane, concentrated on historical projects: historic preservation, residential renovation, and period restoration. Richard Koch, the firm's taskmaster partner, had wide-ranging interests in the visual arts and landscape architecture as well. A workaholic before the word was coined, he worked a six-day week and disciplined his assistants to follow suit. He drilled them in hard work and all aspects of being a practicing architect, sending Barry to meet with clients and assigning him practical exercises in draftsmanship and rendering, the traditional arts of architecture. Koch placed special value in the full-scale drawing, which is as challenging and as difficult as its name implies. His apprentices learned to recognize every detail that could not be cogently described in words—and draw them life size. This exercise instilled discipline, improved draftsmanship, and sharpened acuity. Relishing both discipline and the styles of antiquity, Barry found he had come home to discover his vocation: modern architecture in traditional contexts and historical vernaculars.

Several years later after Richard Koch died, Sam Wilson took on Barry and two other associates as partners. Six years after that, in 1977, and with his mentor's blessing, Barry formed his own firm, Barry Fox Associates, Architects, Ltd., with offices in a structure originally built to house a roller-skating rink—a commercial venture intended to attract visitors attending the 1884 World's Industrial and Cotton Centennial Exposition. It is in the Garden District, the first "American" enclave in the city that still owed most to its French origins and much to its Spanish legacy as well. Within seven years of the founding, the new firm gained a key associate, Frank W. Masson, AIA, himself another journeyman mentored by Koch and Wilson.

Barry Fox Associates would concentrate on historic restoration of antique residences and "new construction within a context of historic regional architecture," as one corporate statement declares. In other words, a Barry Fox project is either an old building resurrected for modern use or a new structure that resembles and resonates the look of the gracious old.

Since the start, the overwhelming majority of Barry Fox commissions have been residences, the plurality of them in Louisiana, and many

Top: Richard Koch. Center: Samuel Wilson, Jr. Below: "The Rink," built for roller-skating, now shops and offices, including that of Barry Fox Associates.

Introduction

Top: Renovation/restoration of the Morris-Kock-Montgomery house. Center: Chase Bank (built as Bank One). Below: Section of Riverside Market Shopping Center.

of those in New Orleans's two legendary neighborhoods, the original French Quarter (Vieux Carré) and the adjacent Garden District. Farther afield, he designed and renovated properties in Pass Christian, the New Orleans exurb on Mississippi's Gulf coast, and in the state capital, Baton Rouge. Beyond the Louisiana orbit, he has worked in Texas, Alabama, Mississippi, Florida, Georgia, South Carolina, North Carolina, and Massachusetts. In Jacksonville, Florida, he built a Georgian manor for a descendant of New England's founding fathers, the expansive brick plantation house for transplanted Minnesotans, and the Jeffersonian tribute for a local insurance executive. On the summer island of Martha's Vineyard off the New England coast, he renovated a nondescript beach house into a gracious vacation home at the heart of a small compound by the sea.

Among his notable renovations and restorations are the resurrected Rosebank Plantation in St. Francisville, Louisiana, and the adaptive reuse of nineteenth-century buildings in New Orleans's Warehouse District. He revived the Dr. Virginia Kock home on St. Charles Avenue, converting this massive Queen Anne Revival house by Thomas Sully into a duplex residence for two families. For his friends Mr. and Mrs. W. Boatner Reily III he renovated and adapted the 1850 Grinnan House, originally the work of New Orleans's venerated nineteenth-century architect, Henry Howard.

It bears mention that Barry Fox's work is not exclusively residential. Other projects include two new buildings on St. Charles Avenue and the rambling Riverside Market Shopping Center on Tchoupitoulas Street, inspired by vernacular markets of the 1800s. Another departure from his usual focus is the design of a nineteen-unit luxury condominium at 2434 St. Charles Avenue, developed for Mr. and Mrs. Harold Judell. Each of these projects was designed to blend into the context of its surrounding neighborhood. While one of the most unusual illustrations of the Fox repertoire was a doghouse done in the Gothic style, his smaller projects have included the upgrading of screened porches.

A notable restoration—and relocation—is that of St. Mary's Chapel in New Orleans. Fox supervised its deconstruction, reassembly, and enlargement on Jackson Avenue in the Garden District just beyond the back garden gate from his own residence on Philip Street. This structure, now a block from St. Charles Avenue, has one of the oldest pasts in the Barry Fox oeuvre. Throughout the city's complex history—founded by the French, annexed by Spain, retroceded to France, purchased by the United States with the rest of Louisiana—New Orleans has always had a strong Roman Catholic presence and abiding heritage; witness its basic government unit, the parish, and its signature public holiday, Mardi Gras, last day before the penitential season of Lent.

In the nineteenth century, as New Orleans continued to expand beyond the bounds of the Vieux Carré, the first Roman Catholic church was built in the new Garden District. In 1844 a small frame building honoring St. Mary was erected to serve the growing German-speaking community. This was dismantled nineteen years later when St. Mary's Assumption, an imposing edifice in the German Baroque Revival style, was built not far away. The little structure was transported to St. Joseph's Cemetery No. 1 on Washington Avenue where it served as a mortuary chapel. According to local tradition, another small neighborhood chapel remained in use in a mansion on Prytania Street, and it continued to serve the old neighborhood until the novelist Anne Rice purchased the mansion. Then some of the faithful in the parish decided to find the means to continue the custom of a Catholic chapel open for public worship in the Garden District. And so it was that Barry, a member of the parish, was invited to relocate St. Mary's onto a lot in the block his house shares with Boatner Reily's, then to enlarge it and in the process to restore it as a functioning parish chapel.

While Barry Fox's variety of projects and stylistic eclecticism might seem original, it may be another trait that is particularly southern, or at least New Orleanian. Witness the celebrated antecedent whose work he restored, Henry Howard, one of the few distinguished and influential nineteenth-century architects who practiced in the Deep South. As S. Frederick Starr has authoritatively written, Howard (with just one other contemporary, Lewis E. Reynolds) "injected into New Orleans architecture a full measure of the sculpturalism, openness, and laconicism that characterized the Italianate Revival." In addition, "Howard's villa for Colonel Robert Henry Short at Prytania and Fourth streets pays homage to the classic London plan house." Further,

Top: St. Mary's Chapel in St. Joseph's Cemetery No. 1. Center: Relocated St. Mary's Chapel. Below: Interior.

Introduction

Starr observed, Howard's design of the Crescent Billiard Hall, now the Pickwick Club, "is a Renaissance palace fully worthy of serving as a provincial capital in some old-fashioned and pretentious empire." Howard's legacy includes "the one instance of a major architect producing significant work in the genre of shotgun houses," that spectacularly distinctive form of domestic structure indigenous to Louisiana and New Orleans. Indeed, Henry Howard, whom Fox claims as an influence, seems to have employed as many styles as his legatee, and, indeed, Fox employs several of the styles that inspired his exemplar, as well as others yet again.

◆ ◆ ◆

While Barry Fox Associates, Architects, Ltd., is essentially a proprietary firm, in practical and some esthetic ways it is nearly a working partnership thanks to the decades-long presence of Frank Masson, whose origins, talents, and character neatly complement the principal's. Barry is the native New Orleanian; Frank the midwestern transplant. Barry is a member of civic and Carnival organizations; Frank likes to reach the office before dawn and work in the quiet undisturbed. Barry is the front man, the face of the firm, the Garden District denizen; Frank, the gracious French Quarter resident whose renovations won six of ten awards conferred by the Vieux Carré Commission in 2004. Barry is broad-stroke and charcoal pencil; Frank, exquisite detail in HB lead and India ink. Notably, both of them apprenticed with the same two old-school masters.

Above: Samuel Wilson, Jr., and Frank Masson. Below: The Conlee house (page 176), designed by Frank Masson, was the first new house built in the Vieux Carré in fifty years.

Koch and Wilson had made its reputation as a traditional firm that designed traditional buildings; this is what had attracted Barry Fox and Frank Masson, who both helped it continue in that practice. When Frank moved on to only his second job as a practicing architect, it was to join the erstwhile junior partner, Barry Fox, shortly after he had hung out his own shingle. Ever since, Fox and Masson have been collaborators whose talents and inclinations seem admirably joined.

Barry is an instinctive collaborator in two milieus, both the man with the glorious conceptual ideas that enchant and excite new clients and the principal of a practical architecture firm. It is he who meets and interviews new potential clients, displaying an intuitive understanding of their tastes and innate knowledge of period styles; then it is he who originates the concept and conveys it in sketches, often working in his library at home just blocks from the office, or on at least one occasion on a plane while flying with a client to inspect her newly purchased building site. His concept is itself often the fruit of a collaboration—between architect and client. When that concept has been approved, developing it becomes a collaboration between the visionary of the grand design and the associate with the needle-sharp pencil as if to prove Mies van der Rohe's dictum, "God is in the details."

The discipline of full-sized working drawings that Barry Fox learned to appreciate at Koch and Wilson is now his firm's forte: the precise, hand-drawn delineation in pencil or ink on paper of each detail that the builder must fabricate out of wood, plaster, or metal—the library shelves and panels, the stairs and stair brackets, the hand-wrought railings and balconies, the butler's pantry hardware. The working drawings of many modern architects on faster tracks are elementary and to a reduced scale, with most details described in written words as much as in form, because so many of a conventional building's elements are off-the-shelf. Not so the product of Barry Fox's firm; its strength is custom design in its overall scheme and in every specific detail. The firm's intention is to visualize the details and then to record them—to draw anything that cannot be described by straight lines and numbers. It is this facility that enables the firm's signature detail in small particulars and its finely detailed façades.

This is not to deny the firm's use of CAD (computer aided design), the workhorse in most architectural shops today and the cybernetic tool that produces most drawings. Few draftsmen work with pencil and drawing board now but rather with computers and specialized software programs that translate rough sketches and specifications into visual plans that can be altered radically or fine-tuned with several keystrokes. Most usefully so far as some clients are concerned, CAD allows imagined rooms and buildings to be looked at from every angle on the computer screen, then altered on command, and altered more, or even to be returned to a previous state at the change of an undecided mind.

As sailing ships are wind-driven and politicians ego-driven, Barry Fox is client-driven. He knows the commissioned architect's first task is to please the client. That said, he brings to the task his own arsenals of taste, knowledge, experience, and persuasion, for it is hard to believe that he would build a house that failed to be beautiful in his own eyes. Consequently he sometimes must educate the client by helping him or her or usually them to visualize their

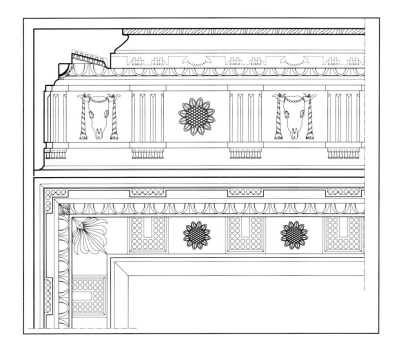

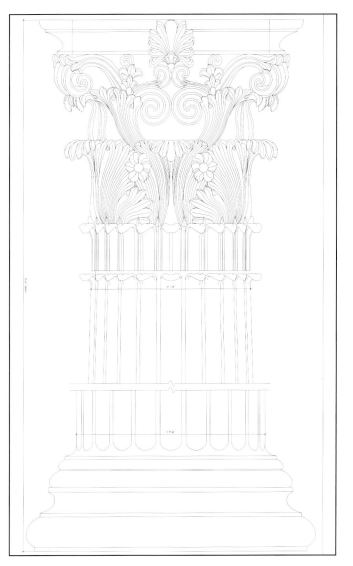

Top: Full-scale detail drawing shows classical motifs including bucranes and sunflower paterae.
Above: Full-scale drawing of column details.

Introduction

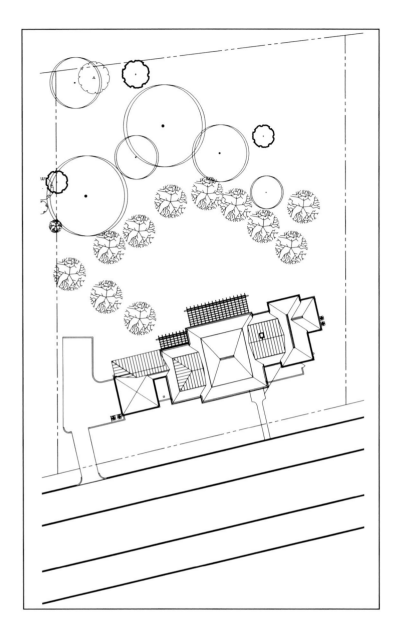

own dream features in terms of physical possibilities and architectural forms. Thus, as one delighted resident of a Fox home said, "He may utterly change your idea, but he won't ignore it," and when it is utterly changed the client is apt to like it better. Two houses, one in Baton Rouge and the other in Jacksonville, illustrate how his approach to a commission adjusts to the circumstances and whether or not the client knows in advance the desired floor plan or the exterior style.

Mr. and Mrs. Allen Penniman had spent a few years planning their new home in the university neighborhood of Baton Rouge. That is, they had worked at length with another able architect who had almost completely designed a house to suit their lifestyle. But he had never come up with the right look that suited them, Mrs. Penniman recalled. So the couple parted company with the architect (pleasantly enough, she says) and sent out query letters to several others, most of them local. Mrs. Penniman remembers that the very first to reply came from an out-of-towner, Barry Fox. Then when they asked him when it would be convenient for him to receive them, he asked when it would be convenient for *them*, and he insisted on coming up to Baton Rouge—perhaps on the principle that for him to see the proposed site and the style of their present surroundings would be more useful to the new project's success than if they got to see his office straight away.

As Mrs. Penniman recalled the process a few years later, she had feared the building would sacri-

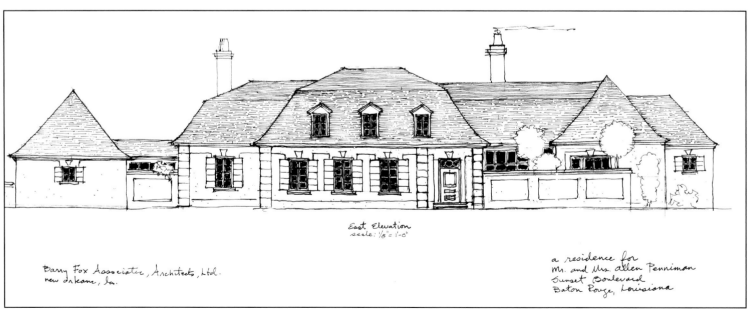

Top: Site plan for the Allen Pennimans, Baton Rouge.
Above: Barry Fox sketch of the Penniman façade.

fice an ancient magnolia tree and the crescent of crape myrtles at the back of the site, because she insisted on having a sense of privacy but disliked closed curtains in downstairs rooms. As for the exterior and visual character, she wanted "a traditional house, but not *just* a traditional house." Fox listened. Then he went back to the drawing board and returned with a concept and a sketch that captivated the clients at once—that looked to them to be *their* home, she said. Fox had placed the house close to the street, Sunset Boulevard, to save the trees and optimize the recreational expanse of the back yard, yet he had achieved the required sense of privacy by adroit placement and size of ground-floor windows. After living in her dream house for two years, Joanie Penniman declares that he honored all her requirements, and "It ended up looking very much like his first drawing."

Mrs. John Anderson, a Massachusetts Yankee by birth, had an entirely different experience when she prepared to move from Texas to Jacksonville, Florida, where she wanted to build a Georgian house on the

banks of the St. Johns River. As there was very little Georgian architecture in the region, she contacted an architect, Barry Fox, whom a realtor reported had designed dwellings in other classical styles there. He met her in Fort Worth to look over the scores of pictures of details that she had photocopied from books in dozens of trips to libraries. Inside and out, the house must look genuinely Georgian, she explained. It must honor the tradition's exacting rubrics—which she could describe from intimate experience, having grown up in genuine eighteenth-century Georgian houses in Massachusetts and Bermuda. Still, she had no idea how to lay out the rooms she had in mind for a house that must nurture her growing children yet also provide ample formal space for her husband to entertain large groups of friends and business associates; and, of course, the house must make the most of its spectacular riverside site and view.

As they prepared to board an airliner for Jacksonville, Barry assured Mrs. Anderson that the Georgian form and details would be no problem; he shared her love of that antique style, and since his

Below: John Anderson residence, Jacksonville, Florida.

Introduction

student days in Edinburgh he had kept the rules of Georgian proportion virtually in his head. The plane was crowded, so they could not sit together, and when they landed in Florida, Barry handed her the sketch of the floor plan he had worked out during the flight in a bravura display of architectural improvisation. Wendy Anderson was dumb struck; it was the rough plan of *the* new home she wanted, and its layout per se—drawn virtually on the back of an envelope—met her expressed needs perfectly. It was hardly changed in the finished house, a five-part edifice designed in the great Palladian tradition.

One of the classical Jacksonville homes that Mrs. Anderson's realtor had pointed out to her had been built for Mr. and Mrs. J. F. Bryan after they decided to settle on a two-acre tract on the St. Johns River that had been in her family for generations. Fans of Thomas Jefferson, the Bryans loved his houses in Virginia, the famous Monticello near Charlottesville and a ruin at Barboursville. Once they had engaged Barry Fox, the initial concept came quickly, inspired by the Palladian Revival tradition in general and Jefferson's later houses in particular, such as Poplar Forest and Bremo. Specifically, the foundation ruins at Barboursville were the rough model for the plan of the Bryans' house. Each of the house's four elevations appears sublimely symmetrical, and each is centered on a pedimented front that leads to the central cupola, which recalls the dome of Monticello. In this instance, Fox's ingenuity lay in the way he made several imbalances invisible.

Tradition demanded that the cupola be centered, of course, and so it appears to be from outside. Yet the arrangement of rooms on the first floor mandated that the south portion of the house (comprising library, living room, and kitchen) be deeper than the north portion (entrance hall, guest bedroom suite, and dining room). Further, between the entrance hall and the twenty-foot living room lies the octagonal rotunda, which has a domed ceiling pierced by an oculus to admit natural daylight from the cupola above. Given the difference in depth between the north tier of rooms and the south rooms, the interior rotunda is in fact off-center, though its oculus appears from the floor below to be perfectly centered in the domed ceiling—just as the cupola viewed from outside appears perfectly centered. This is deft, intentional manipulation of spaces and elements. (The key adjustment lay in locating the oculus askew in the floor of the cupola, an eccentricity that does not seem jarring when observed within the cupola itself, just as a small hooked rug can be placed off-center for emphasis.)

There is a jarring surprise in the cupola, however; the oculus itself startles some visitors who climb to that height for the majestic 360-degree view, the grandest prospect for miles around in Florida's flat landscape. Designed to admit light to the rotunda below, the oculus in the floor is a circular inset four feet in diameter made up of seven layers of glass laminated together for strength. One can walk on it, forty-five feet above the rotunda floor visible below; one can jump on it, though that takes nerve. Getting that oculus actually fabricated took special effort, for no glazier wanted to accept liability for what is essentially a glass floor that must be strong enough to bear several people's weight. Finally a supplier was found, though he insisted on an odd provision in the contract: When the object was delivered to the site, it was set up just above the ground; then as many men as could fit on it (J. F. Bryan among them) stepped aboard to test its integrity.

Another hidden anomaly involves the ceiling heights of rooms on the ground floor. The peripheral rooms—kitchen, library, bedroom suite, entrance hall, and dining room—have eleven-foot ceilings. The rotunda's dome, itself a masterpiece of plasterwork, and the grand living room rise a few feet higher to make distinctly stately enclosures. This arrangement means that the rooms of the periphery are only shoulder height (as it were) to the taller living room; consequently the floors of the upstairs bedrooms are lower than the living room ceiling. Yet the four roofs of the house's cruciform wings are at one level, of course. This uniformity was achieved by adjusting to one common height the attic spaces and the stair hall that accesses the cupola.

Symmetry and golden section proportions were part and parcel of Palladian architecture, and Barry Fox commands these particulars to a fare-thee-well. Further, in one detail of the Bryan house he mimicked Jefferson's cunning, and in another he even exceeded it. In the main entrance at Monticello, Jefferson built twin doors that opened simultaneously; when one was opened the other followed suit, thanks to a hidden device that remained a mystery until its mechanism of chains and sprockets was uncovered during a renovation two centuries after their invention. For this house on the St. Johns, Barry Fox copied the machinery in detail. As for trumping Jefferson's design, this was done in the pediments that grace most of the first-floor interior doors. Another element adored by Jefferson and Fox alike is cornice moldings. So Barry sketched one that Frank Masson detailed in a 1:1 scale drawing to be made up of eleven wood elements. Mrs. Bryan's father remarked that he had never seen crown molding carried even into the kitchen.

◆　◆　◆

If Barry Fox easily accepts the idea of designing a residence that is purely Georgian in appearance, or apparently pure Greek Revival, and then gets it persuasively right, that is not just because the particulars of Georgian style are known and accessible. It is because he has studied and practiced these forms and others for four decades in the belief that their balanced beauty is commendable and still esthetically viable. After all, these are architectural genres that accommodated dancing to the minuets of Haydn and Mozart. If that music still speaks to us today, shouldn't the artful building styles that surrounded it also resonate now? In Barry Fox's view, the trick is to honor the spirit of the style, not just to copy the dimensions and proportions. One goal when accepting a renovation job or a commission to enlarge a period house is to expand the house in a manner that the original builder would appreciate and approve as consonant with his own original design and intent.

That said, it bears reminding that classicism had been out of favor with the architectural intelligentsia, beginning in the early twentieth century with the rise of hard-edged Modernism and on through the reactionary phases of Postmodernism, which tacked onto generic monoliths all manner of classical motifs as decorations, such as oversized columns, pilasters, and porticos. (Witness Philip Johnson's AT&T tower, which boasts a huge broken-apex pediment high above Manhattan—in one of Postmodernism's curious successes!)

The paradigm practitioner of Modernism—famous if fictional—was Howard Roark, Ayn Rand's sort of Mies-Wright-Saarinen superhero in *The Fountainhead*, who declares war on classicism in a confrontation with a stodgy client over an icon of western esthetics, the Parthenon, no less: "Look," said Roark, "The famous flutings on the famous columns—what are they there for? To hide joints in wood—when columns were made of wood, only these aren't, they're marble. The triglyphs, what are they? Wood. Wooden beams, the way they had to be laid when people began to build wooden shacks. Your Greeks took marble and they made copies of their wooden structures out of it, because others had done

it that way. Then your masters of the Renaissance came along and made copies in plaster of copies in marble of copies in wood. Now here we are, making copies in steel and concrete of copies in plaster of copies in marble of copies in wood. Why?"

Why? Because Roark and Ms. Rand's pure, celebrated, form-follows-function approach and materials-purism burnt themselves out in five decades. They were too stark, too sterile in the hands of less-than-genius designers; thus they begat a generation of boring buildings in downtowns and suburban business districts everywhere. Thus Postmodernism returned (with mixed results) to borrow elements that were decorative per se. All that being as it may, as one school follows another, the fact remains that some things are beautiful, and beauty—whether in a motif or an entire tradition—may both inspire and be inspirationally borrowed. In skillful hands, elements of old beauty may be combined anew. They can be "recycled" (to use the politically correct term du jour) so to be used admirably in new buildings. They may be erected in new places to serve new people in new ways, as one considers living the good life in the New South—given that there really is nothing new under the sun. Since Homo sapiens began decorating his purely utilitarian shelters on the African savanna or caves in the south of France, Everyman's esthetics have derived from something that happened before or elsewhere—derived whether through replication, adaptation, reaction, or outright rebellion.

Suffice it to say that in our time there is quite enough new among the inventions that continually advance our lives (and often assail our senses), enough of such stuff that a return to traditional forms can be exceedingly comforting, even stimulating to those who inhabit them. Further, more richly than the merchant prince in Hanoverian London and more rationally than the *penseur* in Enlightenment Paris, we moderns can borrow esthetic elements more intentionally from a wider, longer range of traditions. We can pick and choose as we see fit, and as our architects enable us to do. Thus one might find that Barry Fox, in his own collection of design idioms, conventions, and details, shares the essence of the conviction that Ayn Rand espoused for Howard Roark. In practicing his personal form of southern classicism, Barry Fox of New Orleans sets out to prove that "Architecture [is] . . . a consecration to a joy that justifies the existence of the earth."

Philip Kopper

J. F. Bryan residence, Jacksonville, Florida.

*The Residential Architecture
of Barry Fox*

Farnsworth-Simmons House
Garden District
New Orleans

Clients: Mr. and Mrs. George Farnsworth, Jr.
Present owners: Mr. and Mr. Richard Simmons
Restoration and reconstruction: 1965

The Farnsworth restoration and enlargement project began when Barry Fox was still a partner at Koch and Wilson, and it came to him in part because the client was an old, old friend, indeed a classmate from kindergarten onwards. The nicely scaled house, dating from the mid-nineteenth century, had hardly been touched when George and Jean Farnsworth purchased it. The slightly asymmetrical façade was retained virtually intact, for it had a very balanced look, especially when Barry renewed the two-story cast-iron work.

The interior, however, required a major makeover. The central portion of the house was only two rooms deep. On the ground floor, the entrance hall ranged along the right wall, leading past a double parlor to a wing containing the dining room, pantry, and kitchen. To improve the dining room, a trompe l'oeil window was built into a blind wall to balance the real window at the front of the room. If longevity proves anything, this room is an admirable success; the Farnsworths hung French wallpaper here, and it survives now that the house has its third post-renovation owners.

To enlarge the house, in the angle occupied by a screened porch between the dining room and rear parlor exterior, Barry built a new twenty-four-foot living room with a half-octagon end featuring a centered fireplace. This room also served as the support for a new master bedroom suite above, which also features a fireplace centered in the bedroom's end wall.

Two bedrooms in the front of the second floor were combined into one, while the original upstairs hall was retained. The hall now passes the front bedroom suite and enters a small lateral hall that leads left to the master bedroom and right to another large bedroom with full bath. The attic was converted to a bedroom for the Farnsworths' son, and a decade later the house was expanded again with a step-down den/family room tucked on at the end of the kitchen. Later renovations also included a swimming pool, indeed one of the first in New Orleans with a color other than aqua.

Opposite: Courtyard with pool. Above: Rendering of entrance.

Above: Library. Opposite: View into the dining room.

Opposite: Double parlors recall an earlier age. Above: Den opens onto the patio.

Farnsworth-Simmons House

Top: Pavilion from pool. Above: Pavilion detail. Opposite: Parterre garden.

Trimble Pavilion

St. Francisville
West Feliciana Parish, Louisiana

Clients: Mr. and Mrs. Morrell F. Trimble
Reconstruction and renovation: 1974
Garden consultant: Neil G. Odenwald

The ancients knew there could be no phoenix without a fire; so let it be with this sublime country dwelling, which practically rose from the ashes of Afton Villa, a forty-room plantation house built in 1857. A century later a downriver casino magnate bought the property, which lost its centerpiece when the antebellum mansion burned to the ground in 1963, leaving a pile of brick rubble amid terraced gardens, an ancient private family cemetery, an arched allée of live oaks, and much more. While the honeysuckle took over, the 240-acre estate lay idle as if waiting to be cleared by an absentee developer intent on building one more subdivision called something like Tara Manna Manor.

That slick and sorry fate was prevented by Bud Trimble, who had grown up in nearby Natchez, had skippered a PT boat in World War II, and later became head of Merrill Lynch's office in New Orleans. He and his wife, Genevieve—both of them avid gardeners—bought the plantation in 1972 with the idea of restoring the grounds as part of the region's legacy. Of course, they would need a place to hang their sun hats and gardening gloves when the workday was done, so they decided to make a weekend cottage out of a little pavilion that had been erected in the 1950s beside the swimming pool, a basic pool house really, with changing rooms and space for Ping-Pong. They brought Barry Fox into the picture, and he brought other ideas.

Gutting the pool house, he turned it into a place with charm enough to make the shelter magazines. *Southern Accents* called it "Petite Pavilion; Like Marie Antoinette in the Country." Using fluted cypress columns rescued from the belvedere at Greenwood Plantation, he placed one row fronting the loggia beside the swimming pool and another in the living room behind a wall of glass. Keeping the peaked roof in the central living room, Barry opened it up as a cathedral ceiling with bare beams and ridge poles—wooden structural members which, to the bemusement of the local carpenters on the job, he ordered re-hewn from beautiful old timbers rescued from obsolete buildings. This was the first time he had utilized this resource, which he had seen used with handsome effect by other architects.

For the floors he laid Mexican terra-cotta tiles—octagons with cabochons in the living room and squares elsewhere. Two bedroom suites and a simple kitchen with cherry cabinets milled from lumber grown on the property completed the little dwelling; then Genevieve Trimble took over. In addition to her talents as a gardener and published writer—Barry calls her a Renaissance woman—Gen has a fine eye for interior décor. She furnished the house with French antiques, and so it became a veritable jewel box, albeit one that has been thoroughly lived in and enjoyed for nearly three decades now.

As for the acres of terraced gardens, Gen and Bud (who recently passed away) saw them richly replanted, while they screened their little hermitage from sight behind boxwood and hedges. Imaginatively, within the brick ruin of the old plantation house, they even planted a parterre, a feature that is particularly popular among visitors, for Afton Villa is now open to the public for half the year in the spring and autumn months. The erstwhile plantation, which is listed on the National Register of Historic Places, has become a cultural and botanical treasure.

Preceding pages: Living room from pool terrace. Opposite page: Views of living room.
Above left: View from living room into hall. Above right: Arched allée of live oaks.

2434 St. Charles Avenue Condominium
Garden District
New Orleans

Clients: Mr. and Mrs. Harold B. Judell
Construction: 1978
Interior and lobby designer: Charles Gresham

One of the first luxury condominium buildings erected on St. Charles Avenue was the brainstorm of Violetta and Harold B. Judell. (He had been an FBI agent—and aide to J. Edgar Hoover—and long since the senior partner of a law firm that specializes in public finance.) Barry Fox designed a six-story building (not the seven stories possible within the mandated seventy-five-foot height limit) in order to allow ten- and eleven-foot ceilings. It would comprise nineteen residential units, one of which would fill half of the highest level and become the Judells' principal residence.

The ground floor of the building is devoted to a commodious lobby, storage pods for the residents, and ample off-street parking, a must in the busy neighborhood. The apartments themselves average about 2,800 square feet in size and provide state-of-the-art amenities. As Mr. Judell proudly states, his penthouse apartment (slightly larger than the average) "has high ceilings, handsome moldings, spacious closets, his/her separate dressing and bathrooms, spacious rooms, intelligent layout . . . special lighting for art work."

The Fox firm designed the Judell apartment's interior as well as several other units for their owners. All have the designer's signature quality: splendid interior dynamics, or as Mr. Judell calls it, "good flow for parties," a virtual requirement for people active in New Orleans social and cultural circles.

Although the building was larger in scale than its neighbors, its design was intended to fit in harmoniously with the existing architectural streetscape. The French Caribbean façade with its pilasters belies the inevitably straight surface of a structure that had to maximize interior volume. The exterior of the building is stucco painted a rosy pink. The landscaping features mature oaks, grass, and ivy ground cover in keeping with the divided thoroughfare that boasts tracks for St. Charles Avenue's public transport, the city's second-most famous conveyance after the streetcar named Desire.

Opposite: Façade from St. Charles Avenue. Above: Entrance arcade.

Opposite top: View from library into living room. Opposite bottom: Library. Above: Living room.

Kavanaugh-Rodrigue House
Faubourg Marigny
New Orleans

Clients: Mr. and Mrs. Joseph Kavanaugh
Present owner: George Rodrigue
Architect: Frank W. Masson, AIA
Reconstruction: 1985

New Orleans's first suburb, Faubourg Marigny, dates from the eighteenth century and was well established in 1838 when Nelson Fouché, a free black entrepreneur skilled as a mathematician and architect, built a tavern/townhouse at the corner of Chartres and Mandeville Streets. Thanks to the district's historic preservation, the two street-side façades still suited the local scene when new owners opted to renovate the dilapidated building that had been broken up into apartments. Consequently an early decision was to let those exposures remain virtually untouched, as Frank Masson remembers the project that he began while still working at Koch and Wilson and brought to Barry Fox Associates.

The rear elevation was an entirely different matter, as the ground floor was hidden by the old city's "meanest, nastiest back wall," complete with corroded air conditioning apparatus—modern detritus that was summarily removed. In restoring the antique structure, the architect changed the back of the house entirely, opening it to the ample gardens at the side and rear. The most notable addition was a classic second-floor verandah, which stands on attenuated Tuscan columns and boasts cigar-shaped posts to support its copper roof. This overlooks a forty-foot swimming pool and the rest of the 64- by 128-foot lot, with its mature plantings.

Viewed from the back garden, it might appear that the hipped roof surmounts four floors—thanks to Masson's sleight of fenestration. Rather, there are three floors, for the top level's two principal rooms

share two tiers of windows: a pair of dormers set in the steeply pitched central roof and a row of three smallish rectangular windows set low in the wall to open just above the verandah roof. The dormer windows function almost as skylights just below the ten-foot ceiling of the two rooms that together span the width of the building.

Given its new allocation of rooms, the house perfectly suits a couple who both work at home. The third floor features only a library/sitting room (or studio/office) and master bedroom suite with commodious bath and two dressing rooms. The second floor has a living room, dining room, kitchen, and a study (or library/office). Most complex, the ground floor offers an exceptionally welcoming entry hall and garden room, an exercise room with a sauna, a guest room and a bath, and an office that fronts on both streets in part of the old tavern space. The garden room, inevitably, opens onto the side garden and, beneath the verandah, onto a floor of herringbone brick. This accesses the verandah via an outdoor staircase with danced winders, i.e., treads cut into near triangles (minus the acute inner points) in order to minimize the area or footprint of the staircase.

In sum, a building that was dedicated to a vibrant life and purposes nearly two centuries ago was productively rescued and its exterior restored to virtually its original appearance while its interior is dedicated to newly vibrant lives and purposes.

Opposite: Entrance hall and staircase. Above: The public side of the house.

Kavanaugh-Rodrigue House   60

Castles-Berger House
University District
New Orleans

Clients: Mr. and Mrs. Darryl Berger
Reconstruction and renovation: 1988; 1998
Interior designer: Darrell Schmitt
Landscape architect: René J. L. Fransen
Mural artist: Auseklis Ozols

Erected in 1890, this exemplar of the grand house on St. Charles Avenue was designed by Thomas Sully, an architect celebrated for working in the High Victorian style, embellishing his residences with turrets, towers, and enough gingerbread to choke both Hansel and Gretel twice over. However, in building this mansion for the president of the Hibernia Bank, he revived the style of a Late Colonial or Early Federal edifice of a century earlier, one with an exquisitely symmetrical façade, pilasters framing the doorways, bowling-pin balustrades, and other Georgian devices. By the eighteen-nineties, New Orleans had almost recovered from the Civil War, and Mr. John Castles evidently desired a residence that would proclaim his prosperity (and perhaps the region's) in a manner that harkened back to an honored and idealized past rather than racing ahead in the latest vogue.

Several owners came and went during the next ninety years, many of

them leaving their mark—by lopping off a cornice to slap in a new partition, or erecting, right up against the back porch, a garage for a newfangled automobile or augmenting the rabbit warren of rooms off the kitchen with another cubbyhole such as a dog's pen. As it happened, there had been one fairly serious renovation, by a local architect who was sensitive to the merits of classical architecture. In modernizing the house to 1930s standards, he had preserved the façade and made only one major alteration to the interior, replacing the massive central stair—a straight, two-landing, square-cornered affair—with a

graceful, cantilevered, curving staircase accented by a mahogany handrail. In 1988 when new owners invited their chosen architect to inspect the property prior to another major overhaul, Barry Fox took one look at the newel post and declared "Richard Koch designed this."

So it was that fifty years after his old mentor had remodeled the house, Barry Fox would get a similar opportunity with owners Darryl and Louellen Berger. The semicircular porch outside the front door had always been approached by a set of cascading semicircular stairs; he replaced these with twin steps on either side. As for the rear of the house, he removed the unsightly garage, reconfigured the wide porch with its roofs, and added a balcony—all this to provide a new envelope for the redesigned interior. Where there had been a laundry, kitchen, pantries, indoor kennel, mud room, closets, and more, the entire rear of the residence became one comfortable and many-purposed room: a modern kitchen with cooking area, storage, informal eating space, and family corner with comfortable furniture and entertainment center. In creating the new room, he rescued old details such as marble countertops from the old pantry and original doors, so that the kitchen cabinetry is antique cypress—the very stuff Thomas Sully had installed. And in reshaping the rear exterior, he worked in Sully's idiom, respecting Federal proportions and borrowing its period devices.

As for the assignment of other downstairs rooms,

Opposite: Barry Fox designed a pair of graceful stairs to reach the Sully portico. Above: Façade.

Opposite: Stair hall. Above: Hall with views into music room and dining room.

he left them pretty much alone: the front of the house contains the music room, entrance hall, living room, and porch (which became an enclosed garden room); the dining room is between the music room and kitchen; the library, behind the living room. Within these rooms he did a lot. Because the intervening nine decades had done considerable damage to moldings and cornices, he engaged artisans to repair these where possible and elsewhere to replace original ornamentation or even to make new devices in the Georgian manner. Thus in restoring the living room he designed a new hearth and fireplace, basing its architrave on one seen in Philadelphia, then had it rendered in wood by a skilled carver.

True to the Federal manner, the original house had an imposing entrance hall. Its walls were covered in canvas and gessoed so that the Latvian-born artist Auseklis Ozols (now director of the New Orleans Academy of Art) could embellish this complex space

with a unifying mural of Mississippi River and bayou scenes. A decade after their first renovation, the Bergers purchased an adjacent lot and called Barry back to build a dependency—again in the Federal style—with a four-car garage and apartment upstairs. There is a swimming pool, of course, and gardens designed by René J. L. Fransen.

Because Darryl Berger's profession is large-project real-estate development—projects like the Jackson Brewery renovation, which covers twenty-five acres along the French Quarter's riverfront—he is well acquainted with who is doing what around Louisiana in restoration and adaptive reuse. He calls Barry Fox the finest talent in the region when it comes to restoring and altering a classic residence so that it displays its antique beauty and specific period charms while it serves its new inhabitants, people living modern lives in the twenty-first century and desiring the spaces and amenities to do just that.

Castles-Berger House

Left: Parlor. Above: The bar beneath its baldachino.

Castles-Berger House

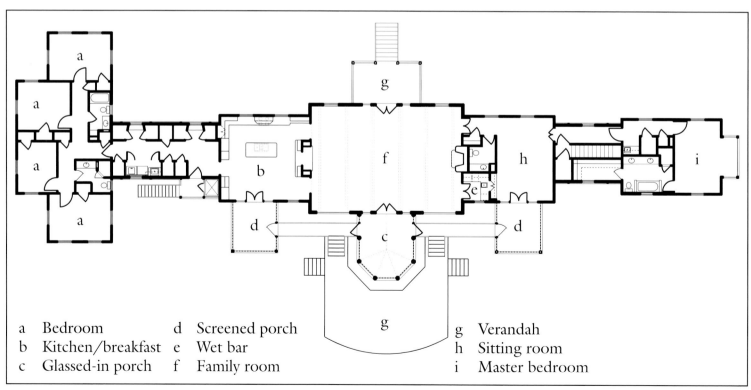

a	Bedroom	d
b	Kitchen/breakfast	e
c	Glassed-in porch	f

a Bedroom
b Kitchen/breakfast
c Glassed-in porch

d Screened porch
e Wet bar
f Family room

g Verandah
h Sitting room
i Master bedroom

Gundlach Retreat
Rotten Bayou
Kiln, Mississippi

Clients: Mr. and Mrs. James O. Gundlach
Construction: 1990 and 1998

Susan and James Gundlach's merged families comprise several children, and now grandchildren. So when they built a casual summer place, it inevitably grew into a little compound of several buildings, a place for everyone to gather in, vacation at, depart from (leaving quantities of belongings in place), and return to. It stands on Rotten Bayou, a tributary of the Jordan River, which runs down to St. Louis Bay, which flows into nearby Mississippi Sound and the Gulf of Mexico. That it still stands is a triumph of intelligent design and skillful building, because Katrina struck here in 2005 and wreaked havoc.

As in many of Barry Fox's waterside homes, he designed the main house to be very linear—the better to maximize the views and enhance natural ventilation. And if this site had a particularly strong influence on the plan, so did the location's climate and the vagaries of its weather. For starters, he elevated the houses on strong, reinforced concrete footings, the better to survive periodic flooding when the bayou rises. Next, he secured the structures to those footings with hurricane anchors, increasing the chances they would remain attached during the tropical storms and hurricanes that beset the region and notoriously carry weaker houses away. And indeed these devices proved their worth when Katrina struck, flooded the first floor of the main house as high as the rafters, wrecked the nearby boathouse, and carried away its roof. But the houses survived, their footings, walls, and roofs remained intact when the flood waters drained away, and the owners set about clearing out the detritus of that awful storm and planning to restore the damaged compound to its former charm.

The main house, constructed in 1990, is only one room deep for most of its length—except in the children's wing which finds four bedrooms clustered around a doglegged hall and two baths. A corridor runs from this wing to the center of the house, a passage lined on either side with ample lattice-faced stor-

age lockers—caches for the children's fishing tackle, sports gear, and other truck. This corridor enters the large kitchen, which has twin arches leading to the huge living room with its fieldstone fireplace and trussed ceiling. In keeping with the country feel of the shingled roof and board-and-batten exterior, the pine beams of the living room trusses are exposed.

A wet bar was designed to nestle cleverly beside that fieldstone hearth. Accessible from two sides, it serves not only the living room but the chamber that backs up to the fireplace as well, the smaller sitting room. Between the sitting room and the master bedroom suite a narrow portion of the house mirrors the corridor-and-storage portion on the other wing. In effect these two sections resemble the traditional "hyphens" in the house forms favored by eighteenth-century gentry in the original southern colonies.

Off the living room lies a large octagonal porch, which was originally screened and was later glassed. This leads to a deck and lawn sloping down to the edge of the bayou, where a small recreational navy is moored, docked, and beached, including skiing boats, sailfish, skiffs, flatboats, and the like.

In the late 1990s, when the main house proved successful but too small for the growing Gundlach tribe, they commissioned Barry to design a second dwelling, a two-story, six-bedroom structure featuring an open stair running up one living room wall to the second floor. This auxiliary house stands about 200 yards away from the first on high ground across a boggy ravine crossed by a wooden walkway. In addition to providing more beds for the extended family, this addition corrects the compound's last shortcoming: It has a swimming pool.

While Katrina cut an awful swath through this region and flooded this site in particular, the Gundlach's summer homes remained erect and sound. There is every reason to believe these homes, cleverly designed and well built, will shelter a thriving family once again.

Opposite top: Rendering of main house. Opposite bottom: Main house floor plan.

Top: Pergola and pool. Above: View of pool from guest house living room. Right: Guest house.

Gundlach Retreat

Opposite page: Views of guest house living room. Above: Guest house kitchen.

Gundlach Retreat

Bryan Residence
St. Johns River
Jacksonville, Florida

Clients: Mr. and Mrs. J. F. Bryan
Construction: 1990
Landscape architect: Robert Hartwig

Natives of Jacksonville, Mr. and Mrs. J. F. Bryan searched long and hard but couldn't find a better place to build than the site of a farmhouse that Peggy's grandfather owned on a little peninsula nudging out into the St. Johns River. Influenced by a favorite uncle who had lived near the famed "Lawn" of the University of Virginia, J. F. admits unleavened admiration for the university's architecture as well as for its founder and designer, Thomas Jefferson. Once they had decided on the site, the next step was to find an architect who could design a residence that would honor Jefferson and his homage to Enlightenment principles in general and to Palladian forms in particular. Strange as it seems, J. F. says, having looked at homes from Richmond to Charleston, they knew they had found their man when they visited a house in the French country style, because it was perfectly proportioned and featured windows that were themselves perfectly proportioned—not whatever style commercial suppliers happened to be selling that year.

Himself a frustrated designer who keeps a drafting table at home, Bryan had tried to design a house to his liking, one featuring a favorite device of Jefferson's, the octagon, as a central element in the plan. But he found himself defeated by the shape itself, as were other architects he consulted, who pored over historical design books and manuals. Barry Fox grasped the idea and made it work "instinctively," J. F. says. Furthermore, on paper he made the other elements—porticos and pillars, pediments and fanlights, rooflines and chimneys, lintels and keystones—combine proportionally as well.

Still, the location was a challenge. To accommodate a basement and garage, and to site the house more handsomely, meant raising the grade four feet with more than 200 truckloads of fill, an effort that contributed to the three years the project required.

Fond of both music and entertaining, and active in behalf of local charities, the Bryans host concerts that would make the sage of Charlottesville proud. The acoustics in the tall living room are superb, the householder says with appreciation, whether for a soloist or chamber group. To give guests easy access to the grounds overlooking the bay and marina, instead of French doors the room has triple-hung windows that open to a height just short of seven feet; these were fabricated in mahogany.

Jefferson reputedly considered circular staircases an extravagance, and when Bryan saw the cost estimates he agreed, so two conventional staircases rise to the second floor from the central octagon. The glass oculus in the cupola's floor was a marvel of technology (as previously described), but another modern device eluded modern manufacture: The exterior columns were built of concrete; then, in order to make them resemble limestone, they were treated in various ways—bathed with acid, even sandblasted—but nothing seemed to work. In the end an older method turned the trick: paint mixed with sand, a variation of another Jefferson technique.

Thus the sage of Monticello has a new legacy in northern Florida.

Opposite: Grand portico. Above: Cupola with maritime views. Following pages: Classical façade.

Preceding pages: Rear elevation from river. Opposite: View from rotunda into the living room. Above: Living room.

Bryan Residence

Opposite: West stair hall. Above: Dining room.

Bryan Residence

Above: Study. Below: The kitchen's living area. Opposite: Master bath.

Bryan Residence

McMullan Residence
Pass Christian, Mississippi

Clients: Mr. and Mrs. James M. McMullan
Reconstruction: 1992
Interior design: Patrick Dunn

The low-lying house facing the beach road at Pass Christian had an intriguing history—before the fates caught up. William Faulkner is said to have remembered the house in a letter; his hosts remembered him for his bad manners. One daughter of the present owners remembered her wedding here when the place was undergoing renovation and the champagne was served on sawhorse tables. So it was for a shorefront sanctuary where members of a family went variously for comfort, escape, recreation, relaxation, and togetherness.

The oldest part of the dwelling might have been an 1840s schoolhouse; whatever its origins, it had long since been augmented, enlarged, altered, and disguised behind a hodgepodge of additions and paint. Commissioned to give the house a complete renovation, the first thing Barry Fox decided was to remove everything twentieth-century. He began by dismantling the house, rearranging its surviving parts, then fitting them together into a new whole.

Perhaps more than in any other project, he let this new dwelling evolve, encouraging the clients to make original suggestions. As their daughter, Margaret McMullan, has written "Exposing its bare essence . . . we learned to appreciate it even more. With the house open and dismantled, we could smell the pine and cypress that were almost 150 years old, and my parents realized the calm that exposed beams, high

ceilings and old wood floors bring. They decided to keep it that way. Now in the finished house we still smell the wood, especially after a long rain, and it's as if the house is alive and still growing."

The front of the house faced the water, offering views from the living room, foyer, a study, and two bedrooms—all set behind a fourteen-foot-wide porch with a colonnade of twelve bays. Another quite different gallery, a trellis of four latticed arches, ran behind the living room facing the pool in back. Rather than have conventional screen doors which would intrude with their appearance (and noise), Barry specified pocket screen doors, like those in old drawing rooms, which slide into the adjacent walls.

The west end of the house featured the master suite with its half-octagonal bedroom surrounded by another gallery. The east wing has short halls, dining room, large kitchen, and yet another gallery. Just beyond the swimming pool stands a one-room guest house, a humble relic from the 1830s and a reminder of this comfortable retreat's simpler origins.

Here was a summer retreat of special low-key charm, an understated getaway in some respects, and all the more sadly to be missed for its visual modesty, because seven months after Katrina, the daunting task of restoring this Gulf-front house to its quiet comfort seemed almost overwhelming.

Opposite top: Rendering of front elevation. Opposite bottom: Entrance. Above: Detail of side gallery.

Above: Front gallery. Opposite top: Rear view. Opposite bottom: Floor plan.

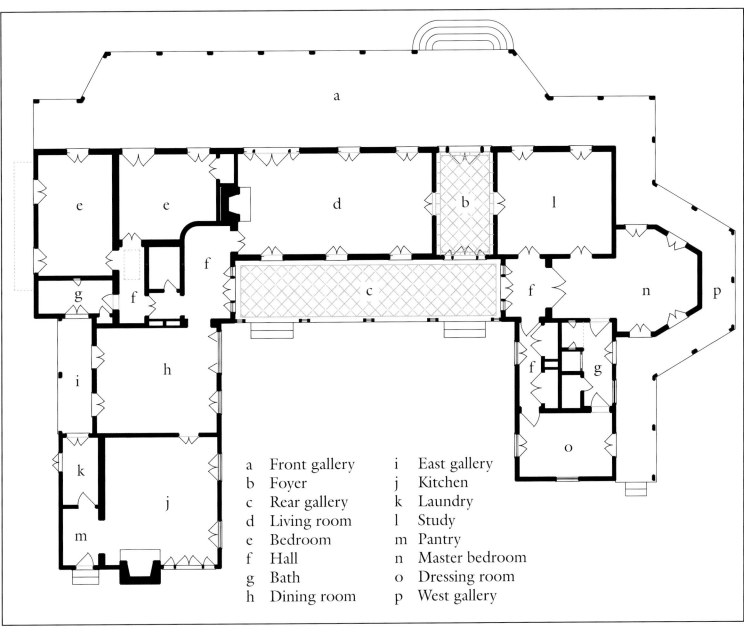

a Front gallery   i East gallery
b Foyer   j Kitchen
c Rear gallery   k Laundry
d Living room   l Study
e Bedroom   m Pantry
f Hall   n Master bedroom
g Bath   o Dressing room
h Dining room   p West gallery

Above: Living room. Opposite: Rear gallery and terrace.

McMullan Residence

Opposite: Breakfast area of kitchen with view into the dining room. Above: Dining room.

McMullan Residence

Above: Façade from entrance drive. Following pages: River (west) elevation.

Ottenstroer Residence
Switzerland, Florida

Clients: Mr. and Mrs. Duane L. Ottenstroer
Construction: 1992
Interior designer: Jennie Stein
Landscape architect: Robert Hartwig

When Duane Ottenstroer assembled fifteen acres along the St. Johns River south of Jacksonville into a single parcel, he and his wife decided they must have a home to suit the spacious property and the park-like setting that Robert Hartwig conceived for them. In fact, it was the landscape architect who introduced Barry Fox, who in turn appreciated the unique character of the riverside estate and willingly agreed to design an appropriate house for it.

The house is expansive, even manorial, with quoins and pillars fabricated from Indiana limestone and a veneer of hand-molded brick painted a creamy white. It essentially has two façades, because the view from the river is almost as important as the approach from the land. The front of the house faces east and has the look of a Georgian plantation, its central mass featuring a four-columned porch and balcony beneath a simple pediment pierced by a round attic window. The river elevation, more East-Indian–Georgian in appearance, provides more open fenestration than a typical eighteenth-century building, all the better to capitalize on the exterior views of lawn, live oaks, an old well head, and of course the tidal waters that often offer glimpses of manatees and the occasional alligator.

The front door opens into a grand entrance hall with a free-standing circular staircase inspired by the famous cantilevered stair in Charleston's Nathaniel Russell House. A short passage to the right leads to the paneled cherrywood library, while another to the left leads to a handsome game room so commodious that a full-sized billiards table looks modest. Three limestone Tuscan arches in the entrance hall lead to the thirty-eight-foot-wide living room, which in turn opens onto the ten-columned riverfront porch. Four pairs of French doors offer easy access to the porch and patio, a nice convenience for the large parties the Ottenstroers like to host.

Beyond the game room, the ground floor of the south wing contains a suite of four bedrooms and three baths, an area that offers comfort and privacy when any of the couple's grown children come for extended visits with their children. The north wing contains the kitchen, morning room, farmer's pantry (mud room), gun room, utility space, and a three-car garage.

On the second floor, the master suite occupies fully half of the central portion of the house. Comprising a bedroom, gallery (with kitchenette nook), bath, dressing room, and his-and-her closets, this suite, predictably, opens onto the balcony above the porch overlooking the river. The second floor of the south wing features a full exercise studio with shower and steam room. The north wing has the laundry, cedar closet, maid's room with bath, and additional storage. Because the property is so far from the nearest fire station, the house is equipped with a concealed fire suppression system.

Dependencies on the property include an outbuilding with a two-bedroom apartment upstairs, a caretaker's office, and pump room, which provides the motive power for both the house and an irrigation system that services two ponds. Indeed the outdoor amenities are crucial to the ambience of this retreat, with aeration provided in the ponds to keep the algae down and with a 1,100-foot pier that offers deepwater dockage on the St. Johns River.

Built for natives of distant Minnesota, this estate offers the Ottenstroers verdant, austral, and aquatic alternatives to their natal state.

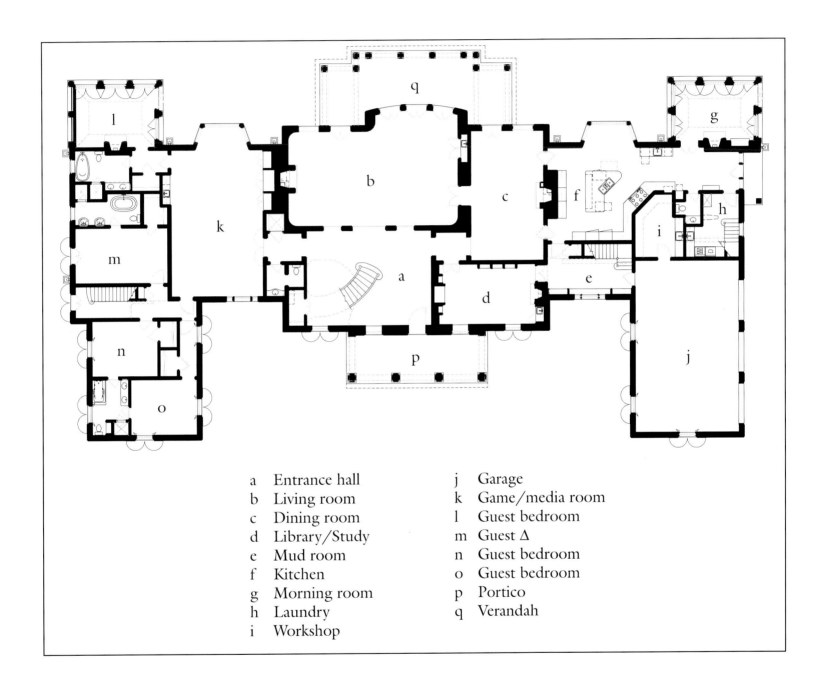

a	Entrance hall	j	Garage
b	Living room	k	Game/media room
c	Dining room	l	Guest bedroom
d	Library/Study	m	Guest Δ
e	Mud room	n	Guest bedroom
f	Kitchen	o	Guest bedroom
g	Morning room	p	Portico
h	Laundry	q	Verandah
i	Workshop		

Opposite Entrance/stair hall. Above: First-floor plan. Following pages: Living room.

Ottenstroer Residence

Opposite: Living room with view toward the St. Johns River. Above: Dining room.

Ottenstroer Residence

Above: Game/media room. Opposite page, top left: Master bath; top right: Guest bath; bottom: Kitchen.

Ottenstroer Residence

Doby Residence
Madison County, Mississippi

Clients: Mr. and Mrs. Clinton Doby
Construction: 1993
Interior designer: Sam Blount

The quintessentially Georgian exterior that Barry Fox designed for Phyllis and Clint Doby may be the truest in his oeuvre to its paradigm. The architect intentionally modeled it on Wilton, one of Virginia's James River plantations, yet it closely resembles another as well, one that scholars cite as a near-perfect manifestation of golden mean proportions, the George Wythe House in Williamsburg, Virginia.

The Doby house is built of pale bricks that have a certain irregularity, the hallmark of handmade brick; these were manufactured in Virginia especially for the project. The front door, made more stately by a pair of fluted limestone pilasters and pediment, enters a spacious center hall paved in a pale tan French sandstone; this hall runs the full depth of the house to the terrace. The rear of the house, overlooking a lake, features symmetrical two-story bays flanking the door, which is crowned with a small balcony.

The center hall plan with two rooms on either side is typical of many early southern homes, and in the Doby house the living room and library are on the right side, the dining room and kitchen on the left. To create the required external symmetry, these rooms in turn are flanked by a mud room and a screened porch equipped with a gas fireplace for chilly evenings. At the behest of the interior designer, Sam Blount, the library is paneled in faux bois, wood painted with painstaking care to resemble the natural grain of New England white pine. Simulated wood and stone, being cheaper to obtain than the genuine materials, were so popular in the antebellum South that distinct schools evolved. At one extreme the desired goal was grain painted so faithfully to genuine wood that it appeared real; at the other extreme, painters (and their patrons) favored an almost folk-art expressionist effect.

On the second floor, the two bedrooms and study use less than half the space, the rest going for baths, closets, dressing rooms, laundry, and ancillary areas. In the master suite are his-and-her dressing rooms, closets, and baths that use as much square footage as the bedroom itself. The latter has a gas fireplace as does the lady's bath. The third floor features an exercise studio, cedar closet, bath, and room for a home office for Phyllis, a successful travel agent.

While the residence's three-dormered historical façade implies the civility, order, and taste of an earlier time, the house inevitably includes a separate two-car garage and state-of-the-art amenities. Thus it links an antique English style with the comforts of present-day America.

Opposite: Entrance detail. Above: Façade.

Doby Residence

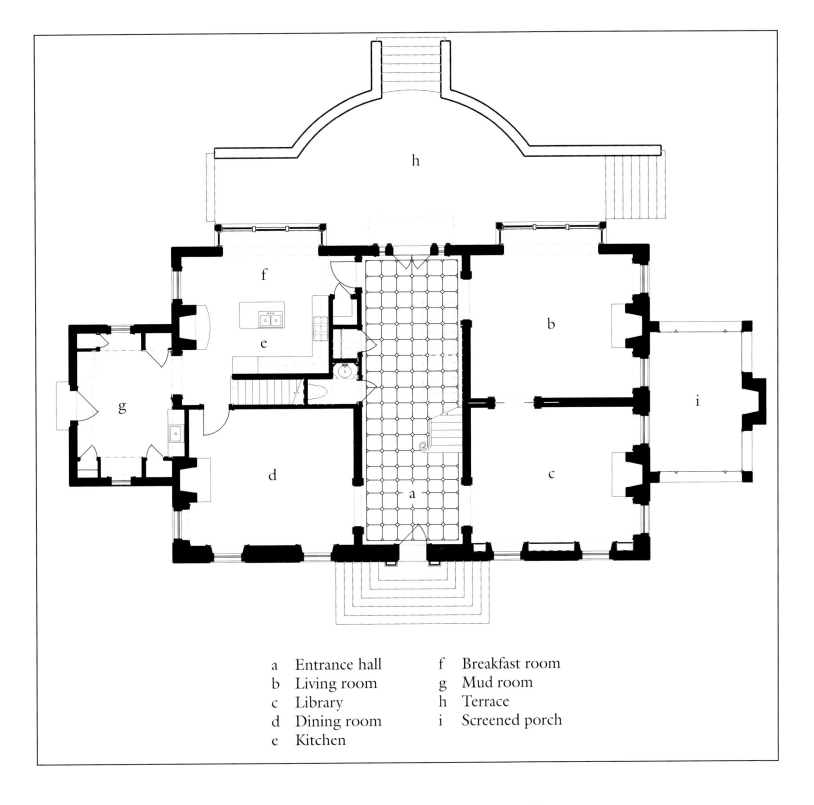

a	Entrance hall	f	Breakfast room
b	Living room	g	Mud room
c	Library	h	Terrace
d	Dining room	i	Screened porch
e	Kitchen		

Opposite: Rear terrace. Above: First-floor plan.

Doby Residence

Boggs Residence

Opposite top: Living room. Opposite bottom: Library paneled with sinker cypress.
Above: Kitchen with bare beams and fireplace.

Boggs Residence

Conwill Residence
University Section
New Orleans

Clients: Mr. and Mrs. Daniel O. Conwill IV
Renovation and reconstruction: 1994
Interior designer: Sam Blount
Landscape architect: Robert Hartwig

At the height of his powers, the nineteenth-century master Henry Howard designed a grand residence on Esplanade Avenue, a desirable boulevard downriver from the Vieux Carré that would fall on hard times and became known for its establishments of ill repute. For reasons lost to history, around the turn of the century the house was moved uptown and partially reassembled. A gallery off the double parlor was removed literally in order to fit the new site, and for some reason none of the interior cornices or crown moldings—elements on which Howard lavished attention—survived the move. On the other hand, the original crystal chandeliers survived, and Danny and Mary Clare Conwill may have chosen Barry Fox to renovate the house because another architect's first recommendation was to scrap them.

Fox took the house "as is" and set about to make it more perfectly itself (with new amenities, of course). First, he cleaned the chandeliers and kept them in their sparkling glory. Next he added deep cornices designed in the spirit of Henry Howard's esthetic

and fabricated in cast plaster; the cornice in the entrance hall had a magnolia leaf motif; that in the dining room has corn ears and leaves. In the double parlor he added a pair of Corinthian columns at the demarcation between the two spaces; and he added a pair of Temple-of-the-Winds columns between the entrance hall and the passage, its extension, to emphasize the difference between the formal public chambers in the front of the house—parlors, library, dining room—and the big informal rooms in the back, the kitchen with breakfast area, new pantry, and very large den with its entertainment center.

As for the façade, he removed the existing front porch and rebuilt it with turned and fluted Corinthian columns and wrought-iron railings copied from Howard's Nottaway Plantation, then added a single set of nine steps descending to an arc of a pathway with five more steps at each end of the arc. At the rear of the house he built a terrace and installed a small swimming pool. A few years later, the Conwills purchased the adjacent lot, largely for garden space. This accommodated a new glass conservatory on the south side of the house and a verandah outside the living room in order to access the new parterre.

The second floor, with its center hall, gained an impressive master suite on one side and children's bedrooms. The basement was refitted with entirely modern spaces: a playroom, media room, state-of-the-art wine cellar, and a garage for at least five cars. Given a time machine, Henry Howard, architect to the nineteenth-century gentry, might have done as much.

Opposite: Stair hall. Above: Porch detail.

Conwill Residence

Opposite: Façade. Above: Dining room. Following pages: Double parlor.

Conwill Residence

Top: Library. Above: Kitchen. Right: Sun room.

Conwill Residence

Dobbs Residence

Dobbs Residence
Buckhead
Atlanta

Clients: Mr. and Mrs. C. Edward Dobbs
Construction: 1994
Landscape architect: Hugh Dargan Associates

How rarely it happens that the realtor's mantra for perfection, "location, location, location," translates into priceless inspiration—except when location means the site per se in the architect's view. So it was with the home Barry Fox designed for Ed and Elly Dobbs on an eleven-acre estate complete with a four-acre pond and waterfall, legacies of a Civil War-era quarry—a surprisingly expansive parcel in Atlanta's Buckhead area.

For this garden spot in a mature, lower piedmont forest, Barry Fox conceived a house substantial enough to accommodate the clients' practical requirements and appear at home within the large-scale landscape. As with many of the suburban canvases Barry has been charged to fill, this site demanded a solution which would satisfy the two-fold needs of views from without and within. Therefore, the façade is serenely self-assured, handsome in its symmetry, with details often delicate, but not fussy, while the rear elevation offers the windows, doors, balconies, and courtyards through and from which the clients, their family, and guests enjoy the prospects of the natural arena around them. These challenges have been set and many times met by architects of country houses and suburban villas for six centuries, resulting in the creation of some of the world's most significant residential designs. In modern times, however, the ancient idea of the country house as a *locus amoenus,* or place of refuge, has been modified, for now the speed with which automobiles and public transportation can reduce distances allows the principal home and the country house to be one and the same. The rural "retreat" can be reached each evening after work.

From the front the Dobbs house appears to be a traditional two-and-one-half-story Colonial Revival design, a strong central block of painted handmade brick appointed with classical details and topped by a wide-eaved hip roof clad with slate shingles. There is an appropriate nod to the southern climate, especially that of the Carolina Low Country, with a wraparound shed porch distinctively floored with a checkerboard pattern of Pennsylvania bluestone and limestone. The wide and welcoming porch provides an outdoor living room in the pleasant Atlanta spring and autumn and protective shade from the sultry summer heat.

The rear of the house draws reference to the prototypical suburban villas of seventeenth- and eighteenth-century northern Europe. The series of arches across the foundation story; hyphens connecting the body of the house to the smaller symmetrical wings; large, semicircular arched windows down the vertical axis; and a central pediment breaking the hip roof all harken to the details and proportions of those iconic designs.

For the interior plan Barry Fox designed a U-shaped house based on the clients' complex "program." For instance, on the ground floor (which the topography allowed to be open in the rear but hidden from the front), the family's regular activities dictated a playroom, game room, exercise room, and guest room, all overlooking a peaceful landscape of swimming pool, sloping lawn, and woodland pond.

The principal mass is a variant on the traditional center-hall plan, adapted to separate the formal areas in the front of the house from the more family oriented rooms at the rear, and it is apparent once inside that the activity level accelerates as the distance from the front door increases. This is a family home in the finest sense, a true and successful blend of needs and wants, and one that fits admirably into the historic genre of the suburban villa.

Opposite: Façade. Following pages: Rear view from pond.

Opposite: Entrance hall into Marsh Room. Above: View from Marsh Room into halls. Following pages. Marsh Room.

Howe Residence

Opposite top: Screened porch. Opposite bottom: Sinker cypress paneled library with view into study.
Above: Rear view from marsh.

Howe Residence

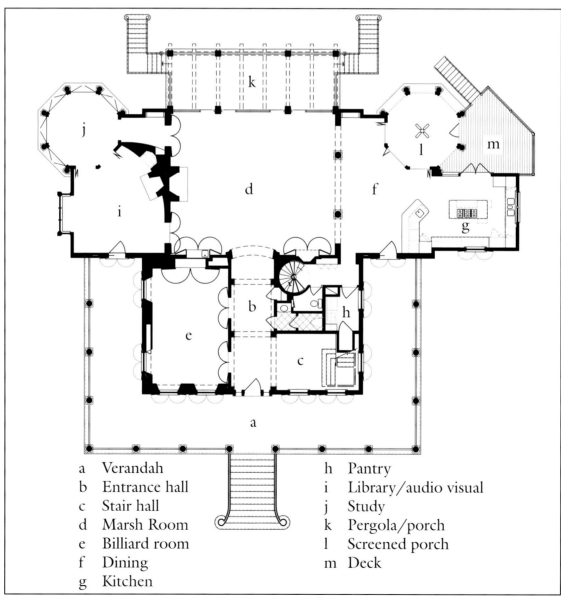

a	Verandah	h	Pantry
b	Entrance hall	i	Library/audio visual
c	Stair hall	j	Study
d	Marsh Room	k	Pergola/porch
e	Billiard room	l	Screened porch
f	Dining	m	Deck
g	Kitchen		

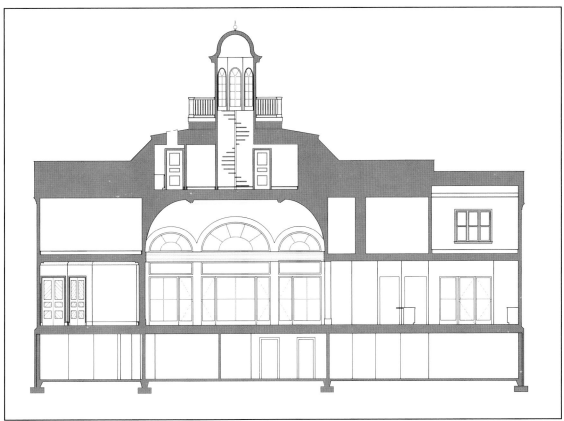

Opposite top: Front elevation. Opposite bottom: First-floor plan.
Top: Barry Fox drawing of northeast elevation. Above: Section from front.

Howe Residence

Opposite: Living room. Above: Dining room.

Anderson Residence

Two views of sinker pine paneled library.

Top: Breakfast room and family room. Above: Family room, kitchen, and breakfast room.

Anderson Residence

Conlee Residence

Conlee Residence
Vieux Carré
New Orleans

Clients: Dr. and Mrs. Jack L. Conlee
Architect: Frank W. Masson, AIA
Construction: 1997

Before building a house from the ground up in the storied French Quarter—the first new residence there in living memory—the architect faced an unusual challenge: How to avoid shaking up the neighborhood . . . not with some clashing façade that would shatter the ambiance, but literally shaking every fragile old foundation, bearing wall, and levee for blocks around, thereby loosing a flood of liability suits. Like that in much of the region, the ground beneath the Quarter is a fluid clay that carries shock waves as a pond's surface carries ripples from a tossed pebble. A sound (or a shock) within this material travels outward in three dimensions, wrecking havoc when it meets anything solid, like an existing building's foundation. Consequently, constructing a home for Dr. and Mrs. Jack L. Conlee—sinking its footings in particular—would require taking special pains and using special techniques.

The Conlees had acquired the site at the corner of St. Louis and Dauphine Streets. The structure there had the drabbest and lowest rating in the color-coded hierarchy that ranks architectural values in New Orleans, which descends from purple for buildings "of national architectural or historic importance," to blue for one of "major importance," to green for "local importance," to orange for late twentieth century (more or less), to yellow for one that merely "contributes to the scene," to brown for positively "detrimental." The abandoned gas station on the Conlees' lot, a ruin rated brown, could be razed without raising a peep out of anybody.

But laying the foundation for a four-story structure made of steel beams and reinforced concrete block was another matter, for this would require pilings. Conventionally they would be driven with a pile driver whose motive power is plain shock— exactly the method that could shake Vieux Carré buildings to pieces. Instead, Barry Fox's principal associate, Frank Masson, specified the use of a new tool that had been employed in a federal project in

Louisiana but never for a private residence. In effect this device is a huge screw or crude auger, a galvanized steel pipe with a plate at the end that slants downward; a little bulldozer equipped with a special rig bores the pipe down into the ground. When the top of one pipe nears ground level, another is bolted to it, adding length to the pipe, which is twisted deeper and deeper until the foot strikes the dense layer of compacted sand that lies beneath the sloppy clay. In this way some fifty-four pilings were screwed in more than fifty feet deep with no more disturbance to the neighborhood than the hum of the little bulldozer's diesel engine.

As for the house itself, it displays an array of forms, motifs, and details drawn from a collection Masson has gathered throughout the Quarter where he has rich experience both as a designer and as an involved resident. One unusual source was the parish's old tax records. In the nineteenth century, when a property was to be put up for a tax sale on the proverbial courthouse steps, the authorities would have a watercolor of the structure painted so that the property could be identified to the gathered crowd. Masson has found more than one bit of inspiration and item of architectural precedence in these paintings.

Given a lot measuring ninety-six by thirty-two feet, he planned two buildings joined by a wall on the long side of the property. Midway along that wall, a gate welcomes the visitor into a garden court, with the principal residence to the right and a service building (with guest apartment) on the left. One enters the residence's stair hall, beyond which lie a media room, bar, small office, powder room, and two-car garage that opens through a single carriageway onto the street. The second floor contains two bedrooms, two baths, a laundry, and ample closets. Reached by the same stairs (or elevator), the third floor has the kitchen with breakfast area, huge living room/dining room suite with a big bar, and a curving staircase that leads up to a unique feature, the

Opposite: Front and side exterior.

Opposite: Stairs with wrought-iron railing. Above: Living room.

Martin Residence

Opposite: Stairs from kitchen. Above: Kitchen.

Martin Residence

Smith Residence
Vieux Carré
New Orleans

Client: Mr. and Mrs. Rodney R. Smith
Architect: Frank W. Masson, AIA
Reconstruction and renovation: 1998
Interior designer: Nicholas Haslam

In a phrase, *drop-dead elegant* was the goal in restoring and renovating this American townhouse in the Vieux Carré. Given that no concessions were made in preserving interior features or limiting ultimate expense, the 1850s residence was a "perfect canvas" for the architect Frank Masson, his clients Rodney and Frances Smith, and their English interior designer Nicholas Haslam, who came across the pond especially for the project.

The exterior was redone in a stucco of cement plaster with smooth sand finish. Windows were refitted and all the shutters replaced—louvered on the third floor, paneled on the windows, and French doors on the two lower levels. A fire escape was removed, a verandah added, and a new slate roof installed. Thus the team quite simply finished the outside of this residence that adjoins the Smiths' celebrated establishment, Soniat House, which is counted as one of the premier boutique hotels in New Orleans.

Inside the excavated shell, the design and construction work was more complex, ambitious, and demanding. While the downstairs remained devoted largely to utilities and existing commercial space, i.e., an antiques shop, it was adorned with an elegant stair hall and foyer, which has a small elevator, of course.

The horseshoe stair leads to another small foyer on the second floor from which one enters the crown jewel of the house, a nearly square dining room whose painted ceiling and four walls of paneling and shelves involved as much detail work as many houses in their entirety, says Masson. For example, the cornice ends some inches below the lip of the domed ceiling which is painted to resemble an evening sky.

The living room offers another artistic tour de force: First the walls were covered with silver foil, which in turn was glazed with a translucent varnish. Then a team of Haslam's artists from England painted the entire twenty-two-by-thirty-four-foot room with a nearly lifelike arboretum of vines and flowers. One source of illumination in the spectacular room is an antique chandelier which, perforce, must be raised and lowered to light and trim its many candles. This task is accomplished by a woven steel cable and counterweight, which hangs outside the room on a wall of the verandah.

The third floor offers only a master bedroom suite with baths and dressing rooms for the Smiths, householders of exquisite taste—and the resolve to enjoy it.

Opposite: Corner view.

Left: Stairs and fountain.

Above: Living room. Below: Sitting room. Opposite: Dining room.

Svendson Residence
University District
Baton Rouge, Louisiana

Client: Mr. and Mrs. Martin Svendson
Construction: 1998

Their Scandinavian name notwithstanding, Moo and Martin Svendson commissioned Barry Fox to design a house with a distinctly English country air about it—an informal house with an elegant look. Containing many rooms, some of them unusually large, it looks deceptively small, although it encloses some 7,500 square feet. Its appearance deceives in part because the house is arranged in a relatively deep series of ranks and in part because the narrowest façade is the entrance wing, which projects forward toward the arriving visitor. This, the smallest portion of the house, presents nothing more than the double door with its wood-bracketed canopy and an oeil-de-boeuf window above the ball finial.

The entrance door opens into a foyer with a stone floor. To the left is the dining room, which one enters on its long wall, while straight ahead is a vestibule that leads in turn into the two-story living room, the tallest space in the house. This generously sized hall is flanked on the left by the kitchen and breakfast room (which extends from the dining room), and on the right by three double doors that lead out to the exterior room of a porch, its roof supported by bracketed square wooden posts.

After these ever-wider ranks of spaces, a corridor runs athwart the house, leading on the left to a guest room, laundry, utilities, and two-car garage with adjacent workshop. The corridor also gives access to stairs, to the library and to the master wing. This suite comprises an office as well as the expected features: a bedroom that is nearly square, with two pairs of double doors opening onto a small open porch, and an ample bath and oversized double closet, a double dressing room really.

The second floor, which surmounts only a small portion of the rear section of the house, might sound abbreviated, as it contains only three rooms. The two bedrooms share a bath; then most of this level is devoted to an enormous T-shaped recreation room with windows facing three exposures.

A distinctive home in a suburban residential neighborhood of Baton Rouge, the house has a stucco exterior. This, in combination with the timbered details such as the wood-posted porch resembling a small cloister, gives the estate a Tudor look. In part, the architect admits, it was inspired by the influential work of Britain's great designer of the early twentieth century, Edwin Lutyens.

Opposite: Living room with exposed trusses. Above: A cloistered porch.

6/1/84   BARRY FOX ASSOC. ARCHITECTS, LTD.   FRONT VIEW   MR. & MRS. MARTIN SVENDSON RESIDENCE

Svendson Residence   198

Opposite top: Façade. Opposite bottom: Fox rendering of entrance elevation. Above: The house from the courtyard.

Svendson Residence

Nelson Residence

Nelson Residence

Penniman Residence

Penniman Residence
Baton Rouge, Louisiana

Clients: Mr. and Mrs. Allen Penniman
Construction: 2000
Interior designer: Carl Palasota
Landscape design: Michael Hopping

A prime consideration in planning this house in Baton Rouge's university neighborhood was botanical: how to respect the stand of mature magnolia trees and crape myrtle that remained in what had been the garden of an older house long since gone. Barry Fox did it by placing the house far forward on the lot, then orienting its principal rooms toward the rear. Thus the master bedroom, living room, gallery, and kitchen—itself a prime gathering place for family—all have precious exposure to Joan Penniman's garden. Even the "land-locked" dining room has a vista through a wall of French doors in the gallery, the other center of activity for the family that can number nearly forty for holiday dinners

As a consequence, the only rooms facing the street side of the house are two guest bedrooms, a foyer, and study (in addition to bath and laundry). Yet even the guest bedroom suite occupied by Mrs. Penniman's mother has a charming outlook into a courtyard that somewhat insulates the house from the street. Indeed, Joan says, "The light is the most thrilling thing in our house," thanks in part to two long hallways, each of which ends at a door or window. The only room not flooded with light is the living room; "but that is an evening room," she acknowledges, where sunshine doesn't count.

The many vistas, angles, and play of sunlight were not entirely a surprise, as they might have been in another era. She recalls being able to visualize the views and angles of the house with the help of the three-dimensional capabilities of the architect's CAD system (for computer assisted design).

The exterior has a decidedly French country look, with both double-hipped roofs and peaked roofs, all of them shingled in slate. The varied roof pitches make the home "a petit palace," Joan exalts. "The whimsy to it was totally Barry." And whimsy was most welcome as she learned she had a serious illness when her new home was under construction. "The house gave me something to do beside worry about my health. I got to obsess over colors. . . . It was a blessing."

Opposite: Façade. Above: Pergola.

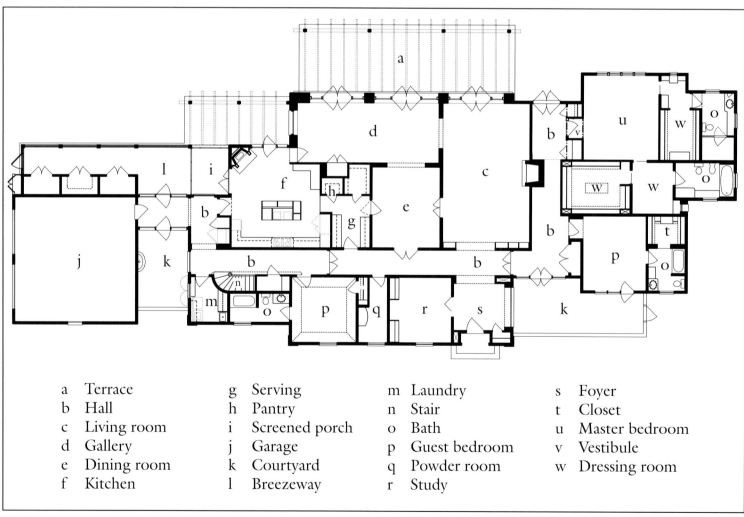

a	Terrace	g	Serving	m	Laundry	s	Foyer
b	Hall	h	Pantry	n	Stair	t	Closet
c	Living room	i	Screened porch	o	Bath	u	Master bedroom
d	Gallery	j	Garage	p	Guest bedroom	v	Vestibule
e	Dining room	k	Courtyard	q	Powder room	w	Dressing room
f	Kitchen	l	Breezeway	r	Study		

Top: Entrance elevation. Above: Floor plan. Opposite: Hall and courtyard. Following pages: Garden side.

Opposite top: Foyer. Opposite bottom: Gallery. Above: Kitchen.

Penniman Residence

Opposite: Guest house. Above: Guest house living room.

Reily Compound

Conwill Hamlet

Pass Christian, Mississippi

Clients: Mr. and Mrs. Daniel O. Conwill IV and Dr. and Mrs. D. O. Conwill III
Construction start: 2000

After finishing the renovation of their home in New Orleans, Danny and Mary Clare Conwill directed Barry Fox's attention to the land they had purchased overlooking the coast road and gulf shore at Pass Christian, Mississippi, that popular outlying retreat for New Orleanians. Just as Michelangelo believed every block of marble held a sculpture yearning to be released, Barry believed that this thirteen-acre gulfside estate demanded a substantial fair-weather residence—and then some.

Before the principals were done discussing the new project, a new element entered the equation. Danny's father had retired from practicing medicine; he and his wife, Adrienne, wanted to establish their primary home on the Mississippi coast. The property was certainly big enough for two houses, and so in the minds' eyes of clients and architects alike, the Conwill compound was born—an estate with multiple dwellings, ample parkland of lawn and live oaks, even a large pond stocked with fish in the rear part of the acreage to the north of the houses.

Barry designed two new major homes as intimately related dwellings—that is, homes as closely linked as the three generations of Conwill families that would inhabit them (given that the younger tribe might spend only a few weeks in spring and summer here). The premier house of the pair, the elder Conwills' (which has been discussed before in the introductory essay) would stand closer to the front of the property and the shore road. With a wider façade and five levels of habitable space, this would appear the larger of the two, but thanks to adroit design, the "dependency," which is set back farther from the road and appears of lesser rank, actually has about 10 percent more square footage.

The front elevation of the main house is Greek Revival with six pairs of rectangular columns set on two verandahs, with aluminum balustrades and a hipped slate roof crowned by the belvedere. The painted brick exterior features such details as jack arches and elliptical arches, double-hung windows, and a veritable parade of French doors with their shutters—practical protection against storms.

The first floor plan is as symmetrical as the classic front elevation, with the dining room at the right of the stair hall and living room at the left. Natural light in each of these two rooms is maximized by a protruding rectagonal bay, a "lens" in a manner of speaking: as the bays have three exposures instead of one, and as their sides are glass, they admit more light into the room. (In Georgian England, builders were more aware of natural lighting than we are today. Their building manuals spelled out how much window area would be needed to provide sufficient daylight in a workroom of a given size for a tailor, say, and his apprentices to work without candles.)

The next tier of spaces comprises a den with fireplace on one side and a large breakfast room on the other. These in turn open onto the music room and the kitchen, which fill the building's wing-like extensions. The first-floor music room has a spiral stair descending into a playroom on the ground floor, which connects with a large recreation area. The ground floor also has ample storage with Dr. Conwill's workshop and garage. The elevator serves the garage level and rises as far as the third floor (but not to the belvedere).

Like the first floor, the second floor has verandahs front and back. The master bedroom, a study, and a guest bedroom open onto the front verandah. A dressing room, sunroom, and a child's bedroom open onto the rear gallery. In addition, on this floor Adrienne's bath and dressing room fill the west wing. Another child's room and the laundry fill the east wing.

Under steeply pitched roofs, the next level is given over largely to storage and is floored through-

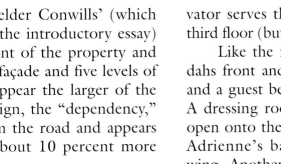

Preceding pages: Rendering of façades—Daniel Conwill IV house on left, Dr. D. O. Conwill III house on right. Images on this and following pages are of Dr. D. O. Conwill III house. Opposite and above: Living room.

out. Here also are a powder room and a media room, which fills the large gable. In addition to the elevator, a spiral stair reaches the center section of this floor from below, while another rises to the belvedere.

Several factors, some obvious and others subtle, emphasize the apparent differences in size and scale of the "main" house and the "dependency," the weekend residence built for Danny, Mary Clare, and their five children. This dwelling is set farther back from the road. Its galleries have modest balustrades, and in all it appears a simpler two-and-a-half-story house with two verandah levels and a dormered attic. Its fifty-six-foot wide façade is a bit longer than the center portion of the larger house yet substantially shorter than the full eighty-two-foot span.

But inside, it seems every bit as commodious, as indeed it is.

The ground floor, which is below the grade of the front elevation, provides parking space for Danny's collection of cars. In addition, this level has mechanical spaces, an ample foyer, and two guest bedrooms, with baths, that open onto a rear porch on the sloping north side of the house. The first floor is given almost entirely to one large living room. The kitch-

en is nestled in the southwest corner of the room next to the staircase, which cleverly corners around a powder room. While the exterior has a classic southern Greek Revival look, this thirty-foot by fifty-six-foot grand hall virtually shouts out its proud lineage.

High up on the fourteen-foot walls, a Doric frieze runs all around the room, its metope panels displaying motifs taken directly from ancient Greece's architectural iconography: the triglyph, three vertical protrusions which originally mimicked beams; the bucrane, a garlanded ornamental ox skull; and the sunflower in a kind of schematic simplicity.

The second and third floors are dedicated to bedrooms and relaxation. The east portion of the second floor is devoted to the master suite, the bedroom facing south toward the water and the bath facing north, with a closet/dressing room in between. The center of this floor has a family room and son Danny's bedroom, and the southeast corner has another large bedroom and bath to be shared by two of the Conwill daughters. The third floor has a central playroom, a guest bedroom, and two bedrooms for the other girls.

An especially intriguing feature is the broad staircase, which changes in configuration from floor to floor. From the third floor's small hall in the northwest corner—standing free of the walls—it curves down clockwise, its perimeter describing a graceful semicircle, to the second floor. It descends counterclockwise then, six steps down along the north wall to a landing and sharp left turn, thence six steps down along the west wall to a second landing, taking a sharp left turn and ten more steps (going east now) down to a point in mid-room.

In sum, Danny and Mary Clare's weekend home may give pride of place and scale to D. O. and Adrienne's Greek Revival manor house. But the dependency skimps nothing.

Today, these houses still stand, despite the ravages of Katrina, which virtually leveled every gulf-front neighbor along the beach for miles in both directions. They look proud as they tower above the trees on this empty, sandy coast that awaits rebuilding and new construction (perhaps under stricter building codes than before). Native to the place, they echo styles of bygone eras; yet these monuments of New South classicism arose in our time.

Opposite: Den mantel detail. Above: Den.

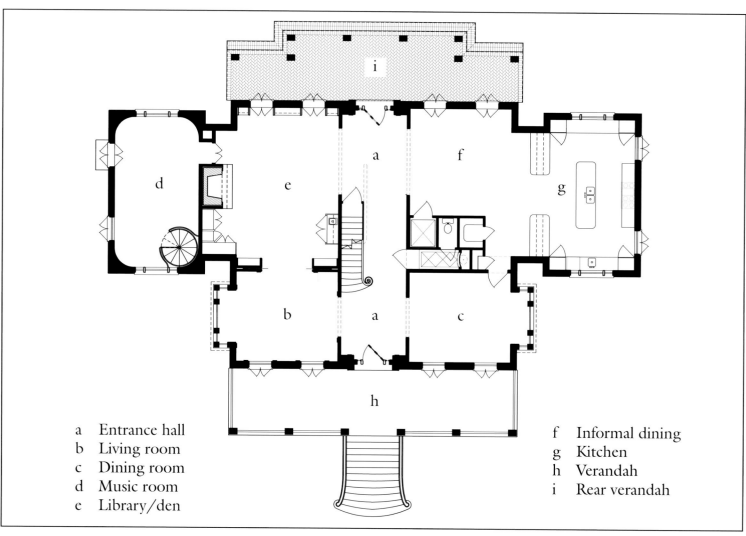

a   Entrance hall
b   Living room
c   Dining room
d   Music room
e   Library/den

f   Informal dining
g   Kitchen
h   Verandah
i   Rear verandah

Opposite top: Rear elevation. Opposite bottom: First-floor plan. Above: Dining room.

Conwill Hamlet

Opposite: Stair detail. Above: Music room. Following pages: Kitchen.

Conwill Hamlet

Above: McMullan house (page 104), Pass Christian, six months after Katrina.
Below: Elevated pier foundations in Pass Christian where homes once stood.

Epilogue

Quality Tells—*Après le Déluge . . .*

QUALITY TELLS. Call my optimism as sugary as a beignet and politically incorrect to boot: Among the disasters in Hurricane Katrina's wake—the flooded city, the ghost coast towns, the neighborhoods become mountains of splinters—I see shards of promise, and lessons.

Katrina certainly confirmed the wisdom of New Orleans' early denizens; they took the high ground when they settled what became the treasured French Quarter, and the Garden District, and the gentle slope up St. Charles Avenue to the university. The homes in these areas—large or small, grand or humble—stood above the rushing waters that inundated miles of the city elsewhere last year. Flooded were Broadmore and Lakeview and parts of the University area, to say nothing of the ruined Lower Ninth Ward. The first generations of New Orleanians had the wit to settle the ridges and the hummocks as high as possible above the inconstant level of the nearby river that carried the lifeblood of their commerce. Thus in 2005 the oldest parts of New Orleans escaped ravages of the epochal storm and its sequelae, the wholesale human tragedies that need never have been suffered. In the case of the enclaves that stayed dry, another adage seemed proved: older is better.

Rank hath its privilege, and to be ranked a few feet—say the height of a man—above the mean high water mark was to be saved. Therefore, it was not wealth that protected many upscale houses, it was elevation, because not all the affluent escaped unscathed. Witness elegant Metairie, where million-dollar residences were trashed. Katrina, the predicted storm that became an unprecedented disaster, was a demonstrably democratic one as well.

A year before the wet apocalypse, Barry Fox drove me toward Pass Christian, the smart, somnambulant summertime town that stretched along Mississippi's nearest ganglion of Gulf Coast beach. Leaving New Orleans, he nodded at some elephantine waterworks of sluices and pipes, eyesores on the edge of the city, the huge hardware that along with the maze of levees was intended to divert and control water. He noted that the Army Corps of Engineers and other civilian authorities had quantified the system's capacity and agreed the present defenses could withstand storm conditions that rated a three—but no higher—on a scale of five. Not a lot of comfort there. Whatever Katrina's wind strength the moment it came ashore, the rains and storm-driven swells from the Gulf bloated Lake Pontchartrain until there was simply too much water—too much for the compromised levees to hold back, too much for the mighty pumps to move. One thing led to another, the rest of course, is history, and so the parts of New Orleans lower than sea level now lie in ruins. Houses and factories and public buildings that had withstood hurricane winds before withstood them again; those that had survived torrential rains before survived them again. None had experienced such flooding, and they drowned where the flood waters rose.

Meanwhile, in Pass Christian and beyond—up Bay St. Louis, Mobile Bay, and farther east along the coast—quality told as well, but in a different way. In the modern real estate market, the affluent are the folk who can afford to have homes with water views, or did until the storm surges reared thirty feet and more to invade the sandy coast and scour inland with forces that are difficult to conceive, let alone quantify. Along this stretch every home that fronted water was inundated; many were simply smashed to bits by the waves, others moved to their neighbors' lots or farther. Katrina ravaged them all—the new mansions, the traditional coastal cottages, and inland behind them the buildings, houses, and trailers as far as the waters reached. However, perversely, older here was not necessarily better. Here again quality tells, but more about wisdom and preparation than age.

Two summer homes bear comparison, the McMullan house (page 104) in Pass Christian and the Gundlach house on Rotten Bayou (page 82). The McMullan house, dating in part from the 1840s, stood just above the beach road; this was the summer retreat that Barry renovated with an extra-wide porch, and a train of connecting rooms—which the storm knocked

Above and below: Conwill houses (page 236), Pass Christian, six months after Katrina.
Below left: Conwill houses from rear showing elevation. Below right: Den mantel.

off its foundation like a locomotive knocked off its tracks by a rock slide. Months later it appeared to me a total loss, its old brick footings skewed, the floor joists cracked and broken. (Barry Fox, however, saw it rightfully as another challenge for historic preservation.) At about the same elevation above the sea as the McMullan house (albeit on a bayou sans surf) the Gundlach house stood strong. Built to design standards surpassing modern codes, its frame did not part company with the foundations, and it stood basically intact after flood waters reached the rafters of the living room's cathedral ceiling and receded.

The quality that tells here is one born of a knowledge of coastal history, a generous helping of common sense, and the wherewithal to apply lessons learned and anticipated. To build in this neck of the woods, one must honor the inevitability of risk and use devices that enable a building to withstand what nature will inevitably bring. Yes, the house was flooded, its gorgeous heart-pine floors warped beyond redemption, its wiring waterlogged, its drywall saturated so that all those elements must be replaced. But the house's basic structure remained intact. Likewise the companion dwelling, the second house in this little family compound, withstood the flood as well. (Its second floor had a most eerie ambiance, the beds still neatly made, and everything shrouded with the dust of months.) On our melancholy trip along the coast, Barry Fox noted: "The structure of the Gundlach house—the piers, walls, joists, and rafters—did not move despite the lateral thrust of the raging wave crest because of the codes, of course, but also because of the over-design of the joist, sheathing, and rafter sizes. Also, the beautiful old pine rafters in the main living room formed additional lateral bracing north to south against the direction of the surge."

Another project, a compound, offered another message. The two grand houses that Fox built for the Conwills (page 236) survived the storm that destroyed virtually every other structure along that stretch of Gulf shore for miles on each side, from the Pass Christian harbor to Bay St. Louis. An independent engineering study suggested why. Barry insisted the grade of the existing lot be raised significantly. The land there was only six feet above the level of the Gulf just across the shore road. "I felt raising the property an additional eight feet to the basement level would protect the compound in a storm like Camille. The rather wide and deep dimensions of the lot allowed us to bring in literally hundreds of truckloads of river sand, and we built a platform on which we could erect the houses. This was done for two reasons: to protect the houses from a hurricane crest, and to improve the views from the galleries and front rooms. Obviously, we still did not anticipate a storm like Katrina. The elevation of the main floor was twenty-two feet above sea level, yet the water rose almost to its ceiling—thirty-three feet above the mean low tide in the sound."

Whether a building is lifted by piers and piles or raised by sitting on higher ground, the effect is similar: a storm surge thirty feet above normal will reach only the top of the first floor instead of well into the second. The engineering study showed another surprise factor in the larger Conwill house: The ground floor garage and utility rooms actually contained flood water—impounded it—in a way that the pilings and footings of nearby houses did not. Image, if you will, a house built on stilts to lift its lowest living spaces well above the ground. When the storm surge comes, waves wash under the house, flowing back and forth like any waves as tides peak and ebb, producing variable lateral forces that provide shear sufficient to cause structural movement and displacement of the stilts. Ergo the house is lost. But in the Conwill house something else occurred. When the first waves flooded the below-grade garage and utility spaces, water filled the basement, and the water in effect stayed there. The footings got wet, and stayed wet, but they were not eroded by the water rushing past and back, so they remained sound, load-bearing structures able to hold the house erect and plumb. Also, several shear walls were built running north-to-south and east-to-west—structural devices well beyond those the codes required. In this instance, the clients' budget permitted a house design that proved to be a saving factor.

Quality tells, as my Great Aunt Julia used to say, without dwelling on how many forms quality comes in. Quality can be the characteristic that means survival in the capricious chaos of a natural disaster. Quality can mean the advantage of the high ground (which a householder might have chosen for the sake of its older neighborhood or tonier neighbors). Quality might mean the benefit of wise construction engineering, methods, and techniques. Quality tells, and quality survives, which is why so much of what seems old is classic in our eyes.

Philip Kopper
Bethesda, Maryland, May 30, 2006